Red Deer

AN ILLUSTRATED HISTORY

Michael J. Dawe

Published by
The Red Deer and District Museum Society, the City of Red Deer Archives, and the Red Deer Visitor and Convention Bureau.

Credits
Hand-tinted cover art by Dwight Arthur, Parkland Illustrators
Cover and text design and typesetting by Full Court Press Inc.
Colour separations by Screaming Color Inc.
Printed and bound in Canada by Quality Color Press Inc.

Acknowledgements
Financial support provided by the Red Deer Heritage Fund.

Canadian Cataloguing in Publication Data
Dawe, Michael J.
Red Deer
Includes index.
ISBN 0-919405-12-6
1. Red Deer (Alta.)—History. 2. Red Deer (Alta.)—Pictorial works. I. Title.
FC3699.R44D38 1996 971.23'3 C96-910769-2
F1079.5.R4D39 1996

Cover: *Ross Street, 1913*
Endpapers: *A quiet evening's read at the mouth of Waskasoo Creek, 1911*

Contents

Acknowledgements/5

Chapter 1
A Point on the Map/7

Chapter 2
Trails Between/13

Chapter 3
The Old Crossing/25

Chapter 4
New Times, Boom Times/41

Chapter 5
The Great War/67

Chapter 6
A Time of Peace, A Time of Troubles/87

Chapter 7
The Second War/115

Chapter 8
Beacon to the Future/135

Bibliography/157

Index/158

For Hilda Jenkins-Hodgkinson,
a wise and gentle pioneer

Aknowledgements

Every history book involves a tremendous amount of work by a great many people. I would like to take this opportunity to express my sincere thanks to all those who have done so much to help: proofreaders Harold Dawe, Craig Curtis, Dennis Johnson and Harvey Smith; researchers Lawrie Knight-Steinbach, Nora Didrichsen, Marg Hicks, Rod Trentham, Fiona McQuillan, Michael Hutter, Trish Buckley, Mary Joan Cornett, Judith Hazlett and Dr. Bob Lampard; Shane Young, who provided maps and artwork; Eric Bundy, Ken and Diana Stock, John Roberts, D. J. Wright Photography, Bill Cole, Carol Turk, Rod and June Traptow, Jerry Gerling, Ruth Stewart, Randy Fiedler, the David Thompson Tourist Council and Dwight Arthur, who provided much of the photo work; Pete Weddell, Craig Curtis, Vern Parker, Paul Meyette and the staff of Parkland Community Planning Services, who helped with maps, slides and statistics; and Harvey Smith, who helped write the photo captions.

I would like to thank the staff of the Glenbow Archives, the Provincial Archives of Alberta, the National Archives of Canada and the Archaeological Survey of Alberta, who helped with photographs and research information; Nancy McMahon, who made a special effort to get material for me from Ottawa; Lawrie Knight-Steinbach, who made a special trip to the Provincial Archives of Alberta; Dr. Bob Lampard and Jane Dale and Frank Winnie, who helped with references; Dorothy Dawe and Allan Armstrong, who provided legal assistance and advice; and all the staff at the Red Deer and District Museum, Wendy Martindale, Sharon L'Hirondelle, Eileen Renick, Teresa Neuman, Morris Flewwelling, Rod Trentham, Michelle Kastrukoff, Valerie Miller, Bev Janes, David Rench, Diana Anderson, Dennis Compton, Bionda Price, Randy Henderson and Lorraine Evans-Cross, who helped in many different ways.

I would like to thank the book committee members Margaret Day, Wendy Martindale, Cindy Coubrough and Paul Harris, as well as Lesia Davis and Lowell Hodgson of the City of Red Deer Community Services Department for all their work. I would also like to thank Dennis Johnson of Full Court Press for his work and tremendous creativity.

I would like to pay special tribute to Kerry Wood, Annie L. Gaetz, Wellington Dawe, G. Harold Dawe, Dr. Bill Parsons, Judith Hazlett and Georgean Parker, who have written excellent histories of Red Deer, and to Ted Meeres, who helped me so much with his research, advice and incredibly accurate writings.

Finally, I would like to extend my sincere thanks to Linda Ottosen, who typed and retyped the manuscript, corrected my errors and put up with me for many months, and to the Red Deer and District Archives Committee and the Community Services Department, who gave me the time and encouragement to finish this project.

To everyone, thank you. If I inadvertently missed anyone, my sincere apologies.

—MICHAEL J. DAWE

Chapter 1

A Point on the Map

LEFT: The Red Deer River, downstream from Red Deer, c. 1900.

ABOVE: Red Deer – a point on the map.

According to the *Canadian Encyclopedia*, Red Deer is a city in the Province of Alberta, located on the Red Deer River 150 kilometres south of the City of Edmonton. It had a population of 58,252 in 1991 and was incorporated as a city in 1913.

This description of Red Deer, written as it was by a dry and unimaginative scholar, does not really describe the city. It gives no sense of the nature of the community, its setting, its people or its culture. It merely identifies the point on the map.

Geologically, Red Deer sits atop a bedrock of shales and sandstones laid down millions of years ago by ancient seas and deltas. During those eons of distant time, Alberta had a tropical and subtropical climate. Multitudes of now generally extinct forms of animal and plant life flourished, leaving a legacy of rich petroleum and gas deposits, coal fields to the west at Brazeau and to the east at Ardley, and fossil beds at such places as Burbank and Joffre to the northeast and in the Drumheller badlands of the southern reaches of the Red Deer River valley.

The Red Deer River canyon, looking north. The canyon is a dramatic geological feature originally caused by the outflow of Glacial Lake Red Deer across the Divide Hills.

The surface geology of the Red Deer region has mainly been shaped by the great glaciers which have covered Western Canada at least four times. The first great ice age began some one million years ago. The most recent, known as the Wisconsinan, started some seventy-five thousand years ago and covered virtually all of Alberta thirty-five thousand years ago. It came to an end some ten to twelve thousand years ago. The enormous ice sheets, up to five thousand feet thick, scoured and scarred the landscape as they pushed forward and left behind, when they melted, vast quantities of debris in the form of rocks, gravels, clays, sands and silts. The tremendous amounts of water released by the melting glaciers formed great streams and lakes which further shaped and altered the terrain.

The periods of glaciation profoundly changed the area around Red Deer. Ancient hills were ground down by the advancing ice, and the old valleys were filled with the debris and material left behind when the glaciers retreated. The Red Deer River, in preglacial times, flowed northward through present-day Ponoka and New Norway and then eastward. As the ice sheets retreated north and east, the river was blocked from its course, and a large lake formed across the southern end of the old valley. Eventually, the river cut a dramatic new channel through the high ridge east of the city, known as the Divide, and the spectacular Red Deer Canyon was created. The river also cut new channels in the soft silts of Glacial Lake Red Deer and the broad valley we now know was gradually formed.

This scientific explanation of the landscape of Red Deer is dramatic, but it lacks

some of the attractiveness of the Blackfoot Indians' legend of how the region was shaped. They held that Napi, the Old Man, the deity who created the beautiful world of Central Alberta, was tired after all his hard work. He chose the Red Deer area to rest and was particularly careful in creating its clear lakes, tree-clad hills and winding streams. He then lay down to sleep and the imprint made by his body became the Red Deer River valley, while the hills to the west were his pillow.

According to the scientific textbooks, Red Deer sits in the heart of the aspen parkland, a broad vegetation zone found across the central parts of Western Canada. Aspen parkland is marked by bluffs of aspen poplar interspersed with thick grasslands. Areas in valleys or along lakes and streams are covered with stands of aspen and balsam

poplar, spruce or willow. This mixture of vegetation spread over a well-watered, black-soiled and gently undulating countryside is very parklike—hence the name.

The parkland is an ecotone, or area of transition, between the forests of the north and the western highlands and the prairie grasslands of the south and east. It is generally the result of a cool climate and modest precipitation. Red Deer has an average mean temperature of 2.2° Celsius (36° Fahrenheit), an average annual rate of precipitation of forty-six to fifty centimetres (eighteen to twenty inches) and a frost-free period of around one hundred days. In earlier times there was much more grassland and open prairie around Red Deer, but control of prairie fires and settlement patterns have led to a much denser tree coverage.

Again, this is the scientific explanation of

The parklands of the Red Deer River valley are a mosaic of forest and grasslands.

The elk, or "Waskasoo," once flourished in the Central Alberta parklands.

the area's landscape. However, Reverend Leonard Gaetz, one of the region's first homesteaders and a very eloquent speaker, at one time suggested that Red Deer had the appearance of having once been cultivated by an ancient race of farmers and that the parklands resembled remnants of primeval farms, fields and woodlots.

The *Canadian Encyclopedia* does provide the origin of the name *Red Deer*. In the early days this part of Alberta was known as elk country because of the large numbers of elk, or wapiti, in the region. The Cree Indians called the wapiti *Waskasoo* and gave that name to the river which flows from the Rocky Mountains through the current site of the city and then southeast to the South Saskatchewan River. The early fur traders, many of whom had originally come from Scotland, mistook the *Waskasoo* for the red deer of their homeland, not an unreasonable error since both the wapiti and the red deer belong to the same species. Hence, the Cree word *Waskasoo* was translated to "Red

Deer" and thus the river and the city got their names.

The wapiti are remembered in other ways as well. The creek which flows through the centre of the city continues to have the name *Waskasoo* as does the beautiful park system which runs along the edge of the river and creeks in the city. To the south are two prominent hills, Antler Hill and Horn Hill, so named because in the early days they had piles of antlers on their summits.

The *Canadian Encyclopedia* article also provides a brief sketch of the history of the city. However, it is only a glimpse of the community's past, a shadow image of the people, events, dramas, triumphs and tragedies which make up the story of the community's growth and development.

Red Deer is a very modern centre. Of its population, a majority have lived here for less than fifteen years. It is a common response to those who say that they are from Red Deer to ask where they originally came from. Still, Red Deer does have a his-

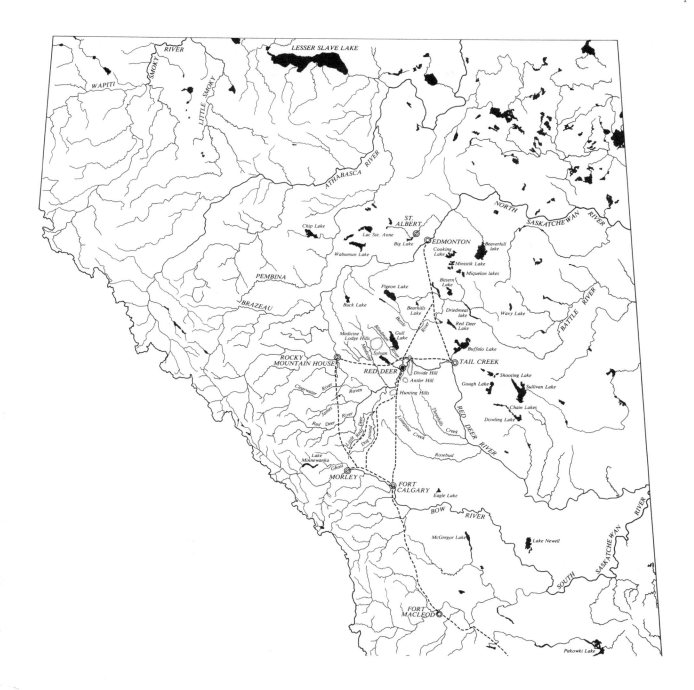

tory. It is more than eighty years since it was incorporated as a city, one hundred and fifteen years since the start of agricultural settlement and ten to twelve thousand years since the first human habitation. This is perhaps not a long time compared to England, where the city of London has existed for over nineteen hundred years, to China, where some plots of land have been continuously cultivated for over three thousand years, or to the Olduvai Gorge of Africa, where fossil remains of human beings perhaps one million or more years old have been discovered. But it is still a long enough history that a myriad of tales can be told and perhaps embellished. It is a history long and colourful enough for Red Deer to be much more than just a point on the map.

Because of its central location, Red Deer became a key point on the network of trails which developed across Alberta in prehistoric and pioneer times.

LEFT: Horses permitted natives to travel faster and farther across the parklands. They also, however, contributed to the increased conflict between the various tribes.

ABOVE: Indian woman with wool blanket and Red River Cart. Contact with European settlers brought profound changes to the natives' way of life.

Chapter 2

Trails Between

According to most archaeologists, the first Albertans originally came from Eurasia across the land bridge that existed during the drier climates of the great ice age. Gradually drifting westward in search of game, these peoples moved into the parts of Alaska and the Yukon that were never glaciated. They then migrated southward into the heart of the continent. How these migrants could have passed the great glaciers is still a mystery, but most archaeologists feel that there were warming periods, or interstadials, during which an ice-free corridor formed between the montagne glaciers of the Rocky Mountains and the great continental ice sheets of the western plains. This would mean that West Central Alberta was part of the great route by which the first North Americans travelled on their way to their new homes in a new continent. The Red Deer area was therefore part of the first trail between the old prehistoric world and the new continental frontier.

The first habitation of Central Alberta is generally believed to have begun eleven or twelve thousand years ago when the last

The once plentiful bison provided food, clothing and utensils to the natives of the parklands.

great ice sheets began their retreat toward the north and east. Groups of nomadic hunters gradually moved northward along the fringes of the melting glaciers, seeking such big game animals as woolly mammoths, mastodons and giant bisons. The oldest bits of evidence found so far in Central Alberta of these early hunters are fluted stone projectile points, believed to be over ten thousand years old.

As the postglacial climate continued to warm, the flora and fauna underwent major changes. The great grasslands developed and expanded. The mammoths and mastodons became extinct as did such other animals such as horses and camels. The new "lords" of the plains and parklands were a new species of bison, which today are commonly referred to as the buffalo.

Over time the lifestyles and cultural patterns of the early hunters increasingly revolved around the exploitation of this rich and abundant food source. Some historians have even referred to the buffalo as the

"factories of the prairies" because of the thoroughness with which these animals were used. Early Indian hunters used not only the meat for food, but also the skins for clothing, the bones and horns for tools and utensils, the hides for teepee covers, robes and blankets, and even the dried droppings (buffalo chips) for fuel when wood was unavailable.

A great deal of evidence of the prehistoric buffalo hunters has been discovered in the Red Deer area. Buffalo pounds, where the animals were corralled or encircled in order to make them easier to kill, have been discovered throughout South and East Central Alberta. At least two buffalo jumps, where the animals were driven over sharp cliffs to their deaths, have been discovered just east of the City of Red Deer. Various campsites, kill sites and burial sites have been discovered or recorded within the current city limits. The campsites on the top of Piper's Mountain in Rotary Picnic Park have been marked by one of the interpretive

signs which were produced as part of the Waskasoo park project.

The Indians left no traces of permanent occupation sites in the area. They were migrating hunters who wandered back and forth across the region in pursuit of the buffalo, elk, deer and other game upon which their survival depended. There was a seasonality to their movements. In the warmer months the Indians would move south and eastward onto the plains in pursuit of the great herds of buffalo. In the fall and winter they would follow the buffalo, elk and other game animals into the wooded highlands, parklands and foothills, where the trees provided some shelter from the biting chill of winter winds and blizzards.

Favourite winter camping areas in the Red Deer area included Antler Hill, the Hunting Hills and the Divide Hill to the south and east, the wooded areas along the Red Deer River and Waskasoo Creek, the Sunset or Medicine Lodge Hills to the west

and the hills and wooded valleys along the Blindman and Battle rivers to the north.

A great deal has been written and much argument has been stimulated concerning which tribe of Indians would have claimed the Red Deer area as part of its territory. The continual movement of the different groups and bands meant that many different tribes hunted and camped in this region. Also, the arrival of the Europeans in the east precipitated a great westward migration of Indian tribes and nations across the continent.

Some of this movement was part of a ripple effect as the far eastern tribes were displaced and pushed westward by the new burgeoning white settlements. In Western Canada the arrival of the great fur trading companies, such as the Hudson's Bay and North West companies, in the late seventeenth and early eighteenth centuries, also resulted in a western migration of Indian tribes. Some of these natives were in search of new hunting and trapping areas where

The parklands of Central Alberta were favourite winter campsites because of plentiful wood, water, shelter and, hopefully, game.

Indian graves similar to this one were common in Central Alberta, particularly after the great epidemics of the 1700s and 1800s. Some of these graves were located along Waskasoo Creek in Kin Canyon.

they could obtain more furs to trade with the whites. Others saw the enormous profit potential of being middlemen and pushed westward in search of tribes with whom they could trade the white man's goods for furs and other desirable items. Still others exploited the technological advantage of their newly acquired guns, metal knives and hatchets in times of war and drove their weaker and less well-armed neighbours toward the western mountains and beyond.

Thus Central Alberta was once again in the middle of a great movement of people from old homelands to new territories. It was also the site of a great revolutionary change in the Indians' way of life, for it was here that the white man's two great gifts, the horse and the gun, were first combined.

Guns had been transported westward from the fur trade posts of the Hudson Bay and Eastern Canada. Horses had gradually moved northward from Mexico, where they had been reintroduced to North America by the Spanish. At first, horses were a great mystery. Some Central Albertan tribes referred to them as *misstatim*, or "big dogs," while others called them *ponokamitai*, or "red deer dogs."

Very soon, however, they were eagerly sought, traded for and fought over. Horses made travel much easier; greater distances

could be covered and more in the way of goods and possessions could be transported. Together with guns, horses made hunting much more efficient and productive, and provided a great deal of superiority in times of war. In short, the horse and the gun made their owners more mobile, more prosperous and more powerful. Together they ushered in a new but short-lived golden age for the Indians of Central Alberta.

There is no record of exactly who lived in Central Alberta prior to this glorious era. The Indians kept no written records and no whites were around to record their observations. Archaeology is unable to provide conclusive proof of the presence of one tribe or another.

The earliest evidence is generally held to show that the area from the Red Deer River south, at the turn of the eighteenth century, was the territory of the Shoshoni, or Snake, Indians. This tribe, which spoke an Uto-Aztecan language, is mentioned by the early explorer David Thompson as having introduced the horse to Central Alberta.

In the early 1700s a confederacy of Indian tribes known as the Blackfeet began to move into the area from West Central Saskatchewan. Armed with guns, this Indian nation was gradually able to push the Shoshoni southward. This displacement was rapidly accelerated by another of the white man's "gifts" to the Indians: smallpox. While the Blackfeet were also devastated by this disease, the epidemic caused the Shoshoni to rapidly retreat into Southern Alberta and into what is now the United States.

The stories of Saukamappee, an elderly Indian who befriended David Thompson, help to illustrate the horror of this epidemic, which was to be repeated time and time again over the next two centuries. A band of Blackfeet attacked a Shoshoni camp along the Red Deer River, but to their surprise, no resistance was offered. They soon found that all of the Shoshoni were "a mass of corruption," dead or dying of the loathsome disease. Within two days the Blackfeet had begun to succumb to the terrible illness they had caught from their intended victims. Eventually, over half of Saukamappee's group died, some by drowning when they threw their tortured bodies into the nearby river. In other camps every single inhabitant was reported to have died. It would be over three years before the Blackfeet would begin to recover.

The Blackfeet nation was made up of three allied tribes, all of whom spoke basically the same Algonkian language. The three tribes were the Peigan, the Kainai, or Bloods, and the Blackfoot. There are a number of legends about their origins. One such legend holds that when they were being pressured by their enemies on all sides (perhaps by the gun-toting tribes on the north, the horse-riding tribes on the southeast and the mountain tribes on the southwest), they split into three groups to guard each frontier. The north group came to be called the *Siksika,* or "Blackfoot," because the ashes from prairie fires blackened their moccasins. The southeast group came to be called the *Kainai,* or "Tribe of Many Chiefs," because each tribesman behaved as if he were a chief. This group was also known to spread red ochre on their clothes, hence the term *the*

The Blackfoot Indians became famous across the Great Plains for their hunting ability, horsemanship and fierceness in battle.

Bloods. The third and southwest group came to be called *Apikuni,* or "Scabby Hides," because it was thought that they did not tan their hides properly. The name was later corrupted into the word *Peigan.*

It was the Blackfeet confederacy which combined the horse and the gun and consequently became the most powerful and feared Indians of the Western Plains in the mideighteenth century. In early historic times it was the Blackfoot who generally occupied the region between the Red Deer and North Saskatchewan rivers, the Bloods who occupied the area south of the Red Deer River and the Peigans who claimed the area along the foothills.

A tribe which was loosely allied to the Blackfeet, but which spoke an Athapascan language, was the Sarcee. According to legend the Sarcees were separated from the Beaver Indian tribe, to which they had originally belonged, when a woman pulled on a protruding animal horn in a frozen lake which the tribe was crossing. The resulting great crack in the ice was said to have forced the Beavers northward and the Sarcee southward. More likely, the Sarcee were a band of the woodland Beaver tribe who were attracted by the rich hunting grounds of the parklands and plains. At any rate they also gained a reputation as being very

The Crees were the great traders of the Western Plains, acting as middlemen between the European newcomers and the other Indian tribes of Central Alberta.

south and west out of Saskatchewan and into Alberta. The Blackfeet, once they had acquired horses and guns, were eventually able to stem the onslaught of the Crees, but the history of these two peoples is almost invariably one of bitter hostility and conflict.

Many of the battles in the eighteenth and nineteenth centuries between the Cree and Blackfeet took place in the Red Deer area. One particularly gruesome clash took place about fifty kilometres east of the present day city and resulted in the Indians giving the name Ghostpine Lake to what is now the quiet present-day resort of Pine Lake.

The Assiniboine, or Stoney, Indians were another tribe which migrated westward into Central Alberta. Originally part of the Sioux nation until they became enemies around 1640, they moved northward and westward, where they became allies of the Crees and major participants in the fur trade. By the mideighteenth century the Stoneys were hunting and trapping throughout Central Alberta and were frequently found in the foothills. They were also frequently involved in bloody fights with the Blackfeet and their allies.

Among the other tribes and bands sometimes found in the parklands around Red Deer and the foothills to the west were the Saulteaux, also often referred to as the Chippewa, Ojibwa or Bungee. Algonkian speakers like the Blackfeet and the Crees, they tended to ally themselves with the latter tribe. They were also generally trappers and closely associated with the white fur trade.

By the mid-1700s the Hudson's Bay Company found that the various tribes of Indians were becoming increasingly reluctant to make the long trip to the Hudson Bay to trade their furs, preferring instead to trade with others who established posts closer to their hunting grounds. The Hudson's Bay Company's first reaction was to send emissaries inland to try to entice the Indians to return to the Bay.

fierce and warlike, and they usually hunted and traded with the Bloods and the Peigans.

Another tribe, which at one time had been allied with the Blackfeet, were the Atsina, or Gros Ventre, from a French term meaning "big bellies." This tribe had once been part of the Arapaho tribe and had gradually migrated in the eighteenth century from West Central Saskatchewan into Central and Southern Alberta. The Atsina were famous for their uneasy and sometimes violent relationship with the white fur traders. In the midnineteenth century they also had a violent quarrel with the Blackfeet and eventually moved into what is now the United States.

The Cree, one of the largest tribes in all of Canada, was also one of the first groups to be in contact with the white fur traders. The Cree were one of the tribes to see the advantage of being middlemen and were frequent traders with other tribes. They also used the weapons they acquired from the whites to push tribes such as the Blackfeet

In 1754 the company dispatched Anthony Henday on such a quest. In September he became the first European to travel into what is now the Province of Alberta. In mid-October Henday had his historic first meeting with the Blackfeet at a large encampment of over 1,500 tribesmen near Pine Lake. However, he was unsuccessful in his mission to convince them of the desirability of making a long trip to the Hudson Bay.

Henday continued his travels through the region. Many people believe that it was at a site on or near Antler Hill, just south of the City of Red Deer, that he became the first European to view the Rocky Mountains. Henday spent the winter of 1754–1755 hunting and trapping in the parklands and forest west of Red Deer. In the spring he returned to the Hudson Bay.

Henday, in the company of another fur trader, Joseph Smith, returned to Central Alberta in 1759 and again spent another winter in the country west of Red Deer. Several other explorers also travelled through Central Alberta in subsequent years. One of these, Peter Fidler, was also a surveyor, and in 1792 he made the first compass bearings on the Rocky Mountains from a site just east of present-day Red Deer. David Thompson was also a surveyor and an outstanding cartographer, and it was he who made the first accurate maps of Central Alberta.

By the latter part of the eighteenth century, the Hudson's Bay Company had finally realized the folly of its old trading practices, and it joined its great rival, the North West Company, in a competition to build posts inland along such rivers as the North Saskatchewan. In 1795 both companies built posts near the current site of Edmonton, and in 1799 the North West Company built Rocky Mountain House and the Hudson's Bay Company constructed Acton House ninety kilometres west of Red Deer near the confluence of the North Saskatchewan and Clearwater rivers.

This development had a major impact on the patterns of movement in the Red Deer area. The various bands of Indians now frequently travelled through the area on their way north to the posts at Edmonton or west toward Rocky Mountain House. Over time, three broad routes developed. One followed the foothills through

The courageous Father Albert Lacombe, affectionately known as Goodheart, ministered to the native and Métis people of Alberta for more than sixty years. The town of Lacombe, just north of Red Deer, is named in his honour.

the natives had little or no resistance, devastated the region. The measles epidemic of 1819–1820 wiped out an estimated one-third of the Blackfeet and Atsina tribes. A diphtheria epidemic in 1836 killed many of the children, and in 1837 one of the worst epidemics, an outbreak of smallpox, had an almost unimaginable impact on the tribes. Over two-thirds of the Blackfeet tribes perished, and the Sarcee tribe was reduced to a mere 250 natives.

In the midnineteenth century another important development took place with the arrival of the first missionaries. The earliest of these was a Wesleyan Methodist by the name of Robert Terrill Rundle. In 1841 Rundle first travelled through the area when he visited Rocky Mountain House and Cree, Assiniboine and Blackfoot Indian camps near the current site of Red Deer. During that visit he had the horrifying experience of witnessing a double murder a short distance from his tent and then being forced by circumstances, two days later, to spend the night in the same tent as the murderers.

In 1842 Father Jean Baptiste Thibeault visited Rocky Mountain House. Other early missionaries to travel through Central Alberta in subsequent years were Father Pierre de Smet, a Jesuit, and Thomas Woolsey, a Methodist.

One of the most famous of the early missionaries was Father Albert Lacombe, who arrived in Alberta in 1852 and made his first trip to the parklands of Central Alberta in the spring of 1855. A few years later Father Lacombe made a trip eastward from Rocky Mountain House to visit the Blood, Peigan and Blackfoot camps around the present site of Red Deer and north along the Battle River. One night a Cree war party struck the camp where Father Lacombe was staying and a terrible battle ensued. During the slaughter Lacombe tried to stop the fighting by walking directly into the attackers' line of fire. He was wounded in the head and shoulder, but fortunately survived.

the Rocky Mountain House area while another passed through the prairie regions to the east around Buffalo Lake. The central route, the one through the Red Deer area, became known to some as the Blackfoot Trail or the Wolf Track. Again, this area of Alberta became part of a "trail between."

The early 1800s were times of prosperity for the Indian inhabitants of Central Alberta, but they were also times of great tragedy. Terrible epidemics such as smallpox, measles, diphtheria, scarlet fever and others, to which

The Crees, disheartened and guilty over what they had just done, fell back in retreat and the battle suddenly ended.

Two of the most famous Methodist missionaries, George McDougall and his son John, arrived in Alberta in 1862 on the first a great many trips they were to make through the Red Deer area over the next several years. On one particularly eventful journey the McDougalls were shooting ducks in the canyon just east of Red Deer. John accidentally dropped his gun with the result that his father was seriously wounded in the chest and legs. John and his companion, Peter Erasmus, did what they could to treat the elder McDougall, and while they were waiting for him to recuperate, they panned for gold using one of their frying pans. They found what they felt were promising colours, but decided that since the area was part of a "theatre of constant tribal war, a small party would not be safe to work here very long." Fortunately, they were not attacked by hostile natives, and George McDougall soon recovered sufficiently to allow them to return home.

In 1873 the McDougalls established a mission at Morley in the foothills of Southwestern Alberta. In October of that year they cut a 450-kilometre-long cart trail from Fort Edmonton to the new mission. This trail followed the old Wolf Track south to the ford on the Red Deer River, three kilometres upstream from the current city limits, and then southward across the prairie to the foothills along the Bow River. The old foot and horse path of the Indians and fur traders had become a definite trail between the fur trade posts of the north and a mission of the south.

A good friend of the McDougalls was the famous Cree chief Maskepetoon, who became renowned for his attempts to end the incessant fighting between the Crees and the Blackfeet. Maskepetoon frequently camped in the Red Deer area. The Peace Hills, ninety kilometres to the north, commemorate one of the accords which he helped to negotiate. Tragically, in 1869, Maskepetoon was murdered while on one of his peace missions by a young Blackfoot warrior. The park on the western edge of the city was named in honour of this great peacemaker, as was Great Chief Park.

The latter half of the nineteenth century saw a number of other significant developments and events. In 1857 the British government commissioned Sir John Palliser to lead a major exploration of the western plains and parklands in order to determine their resource and settlement potential. For the first time the Canadian West was being considered by whites from a perspective other than that of an "uncivilized" land of fur traders, Indians and a handful of missionaries.

Palliser's reports provide an outstanding description of the current site of Red Deer and surrounding area which

TOP: The Reverend George McDougall.

ABOVE: The Reverend John McDougall.

The McDougalls, pioneer missionaries, were frequent visitors to Central Alberta and cut a cart trail through the Red Deer area from Fort Edmonton to the Morley Mission west of Calgary in 1873.

LEFT: Maskepetoon, dubbed the Great Chief by Kerry Wood in his award-winning book of the same name, became famous for his efforts to bring peace between the Blackfoot and the Cree.

A group of Crees and Métis on the McKenzie Trail, south of Red Deer near Antler Hill. The trail was named after early Métis settlers and provided an easterly alternate route to the Calgary–Edmonton Trail.

the expedition visited in July 1858. The explorers found coal burning in the banks of the Red Deer River downstream from the present-day city. They got their first view of the Rocky Mountains from the "Nick," a spot just south of the present-day Coal Trail where it crosses the Divide Hill. They noted the damage which a hailstorm had inflicted on the smaller plants and grasses, and lamented over the destruction by prairie fire of the stands of balsam poplar in the valley.

The reports of the Palliser expedition also noted that the vast herds of buffalo in Western Canada were beginning to vanish. One early consequence of this development was the arrival in Central Alberta of large groups of Métis, a people whose origins stemmed from the intermarriage of the white fur traders and the native Indians. These Métis had formerly hunted buffalo out of the settlements along the Red River of Manitoba, but as the herds began to shrink, they had been forced to travel farther and farther west. They were soon joined in their hunts by other Métis from the fur trade posts and tiny mission settlements to the north. By the 1860s and early 1870s, large semipermanent buffalo hunting camps had formed east of Red Deer around Buffalo Lake and the confluence of Tail Creek and the Red Deer River. At one time these communities had as many as 2,000 residents. The records of the Half-breed Land Claims Commission in the National Archives of Canada suggest that

there may have also been smaller Métis settlements near the confluence of the Blindman and Red Deer rivers.

These settlements regrettably helped to attract to Central Alberta a new scourge: whiskey traders from the United States. The liquor which they sold was often barely deserving of such a designation because it was frequently a poisonous concoction of tobacco, molasses, old tea leaves, red ink, patent medicine and alcohol. The immense profits they made impoverished the Indians and the Métis. The whole era was marked by terrible suffering and death.

These tortured times were made worse by the accelerating disappearance of the buffalo, the staple upon which Central Alberta's inhabitants depended, and by another outbreak of the dreaded smallpox. In this epidemic of 1870, an estimated one-half of the Indians of Alberta perished along with several hundred Métis. A small graveyard, which formerly stood just west of where present-day Highway 2 crosses the Red Deer River, contained the graves of some of those who died from this terrible disease.

The state of things became so serious that even the distant federal government in Ottawa took notice. In 1874 the North West Mounted Police were sent to Western Canada to restore law and order and end the whiskey trade. In 1875 a small police post was established at Tail Creek to ensure the end of lawlessness in Central Alberta. The construction by the police of Fort Calgary on the Bow

River also led to the establishment of a new Hudson's Bay Company trading post at that location and the closure of the unprofitable post at Rocky Mountain House.

The Indian tribes, recognizing that their old way of life was rapidly coming to an end, agreed to sign treaties with the government. By these agreements they surrendered their rights to their old hunting grounds in exchange for reserves based on a population of five persons per square mile, annuity payments and other benefits such as assistance in education, farming and health care. In 1876 the Crees signed Treaty Number Six. The following year the Blackfeet, Sarcee and Stoneys signed Treaty Number Seven. The dividing line between the areas covered by these two treaties was the Red Deer River as far east as the Buffalo Lake country. It generally reflected the territorial division between the Cree and the Blackfeet tribes as it had evolved by the 1870s.

By 1880 reserves had been established both north and south of Red Deer. The Crees and Stoneys received lands near present-day Hobbema and Ponoka, while the Blackfoot Reserve was set 100 kilometres east of Fort Calgary, the Peigan Reserve west of Fort Macleod and the Mountain Stoney Reserve around Morley. Perhaps because Red Deer was in the middle of the borderlands, no reserve was established near the present city.

Unfortunately, by 1880, the buffalo had completely vanished. The Indians, for whom the government had expected the buffalo to provide sustenance for at least a few more years, were largely left starving and destitute. A few highly independent bands continued to try to eke out an existence off the reserves. While they were usually found in either the Buffalo Lake country or in the western foothills, they often wandered through the area around Red Deer for several more years. Because the government usually refused to give them even the meagre rations that were provided to those on the reserves, their lives were generally very hard and often desperate.

In 1880 the settlements to the north such as Fort Edmonton and the mission of St. Albert, and the new settlements to the south at the police posts of Fort Calgary and Fort Macleod, had begun to bud and grow. The trail through Red Deer was increasingly used by another breed of pioneer, freighters travelling north from Montana and Southern Alberta and south from Fort Edmonton. The Red Deer area was entering a new era, and its development would be shaped by its new role as a point on the freight trail between Northern and Southern Alberta.

The ruins of Rocky Mountain House photographed by the famous J.B. Tyrrell in 1886. Such early photographs chronicled the passing of a way of life in Western Canada.

Chapter 3

The Old Crossing

LEFT: The Red Deer Crossing settlement as it appeared in the spring of 1886. In the foreground is the Calgary–Edmonton Trail. To the left is Fort Normandeau and on the right is Robert McClellan's farmstead.

ABOVE: Addison McPherson, the colourful frontiersman, freighter and first settler at the Red Deer Crossing.

Travel through Central Alberta in the 1870s and 1880s was no easy matter. In summertime, travellers could face oppressive heat, drenching rain, sudden hailstorms, seas of mud, choking dust or clouds of biting insects. In wintertime trails could be blocked by heavy snows and drifts, or obscured by ice fogs or blinding blizzards. The brutal cold could literally threaten life and limb. Even the famous Chinooks, the usually welcome warm winds of winter, could play havoc by making sleighing difficult if not impossible.

Rivers and streams were special hazards. During fall freeze-up or spring breakup, it was extremely dangerous to cross the ice. Spring and summer floods could sweep away everything in their paths and make crossings impossible. Even at the best of times, getting across a river was a wet and unpleasant experience.

It is therefore not surprising that travellers sought out the places where the water was shallower and easier to cross. One such spot was to be found three kilometres upstream from the current city limits, where a shelf of sandstone provided a shallow

The Red Deer Crossing was the best and safest ford across the Red Deer River for a distance of 100 kilometres and hence was a strategic link between Northern and Southern Alberta.

crossing point. It was the best and safest ford for a distance of over fifty kilometres in either direction.

The popularity of this ford was greatly enhanced by its strategic location between the settlements of Northern Alberta and the police posts and missions of the South. If a straight line were to be drawn between Fort Calgary and Fort Edmonton, this crossing would be a mere six kilometres west of that line's intersection with the Red Deer River. Moreover, the ford was nearly equidistant between those two communities. It was therefore a key link on the emerging transportation backbone of Alberta: the Calgary–Edmonton Trail.

This ford had been used by the McDougalls when they cut their cart trail from Fort Edmonton to the Morley Mission in 1873. As a result some people referred to it as McDougall's Crossing. Others called it the Wolf's Crossing because it was on the south end of the old Wolf Track. More commonly, it was referred to as the Red Deer Crossing, or simply, the Crossing.

Travel over the Calgary–Edmonton Trail was generally slow and arduous. It would often take anywhere from ten to fifteen days to cover the whole 350 kilometre length of the trail. Consequently, travellers had to make frequent overnight stops. The Red Deer Crossing, with its good shelter and ample supplies of firewood and water, became one of the favourite campsites.

The first non-native habitation to be constructed at the Crossing was a small shack, built and intermittently used by Addison McPherson. A native of Virginia, McPherson was a true frontiersman who came to Alberta from Montana in 1869. Together with his partner, Charlie Smith, McPherson made his way by hunting buffalo, trapping for furs, poisoning wolves for their pelts, trading with the Indians and prospecting for gold. It was while he was engaged in this latter activity that McPherson built his log shack at the Crossing in either 1869 or, more probably, in 1872.

A good indication of McPherson's character can be gained from a quarrel he had with the famous Sarcee chief Bull Head. McPherson pulled his gun on the bellicose Bull Head when the chief made an attempt to grab his small supply of tobacco. Fortunately, for McPherson, the Sarcees decided to retaliate, not by killing him, but rather by seizing the carcasses of the several hundred wolves he and his partner had poisoned. Undaunted, McPherson made his way up to Fort Edmonton, where he purchased a sizeable quantity of tobacco. He then returned to the Sarcees' camp and made a gift of it without mentioning anything about the wolves. By the end of the next day the astonished Indians had skinned all the carcasses and neatly stacked the pelts behind McPherson's cabin. He boasted to his friends that the whole venture had cost him

a fraction of what he would have gladly paid to have the work done.

In 1875 McPherson hauled a load of furs and buffalo hides to Winnipeg. On his return he hauled a load of goods to Fort Edmonton and thus commenced a freighting operation which was ultimately to be one of the largest in all of Western Canada. Soon his outfits joined the others making their way up and down the Calgary—Edmonton Trail.

As the 1870s turned to a new decade, the growing volume of traffic on the trail through the Red Deer Crossing made it obvious that McPherson's tiny shack would soon be joined by the more permanent homes and claims of those wishing to start new lives in the parkland. This was an eventuality made even more certain by the plan to construct the Canadian Pacific Railroad (CPR) across the prairies and by the land policies of the federal government.

Shortly after McPherson's arrival in Central Alberta, the government established a procedure called homesteading, by which a settler could obtain free title to one-quarter section of land (160 acres), provided that he fulfilled certain registration, residency and land improvement requirements. It was a lure which was soon to draw thousands to the Canadian West.

An important adjunct to the government's homestead policy was its land division policy. The entire Canadian West was to be subdivided into square mile sections of land arranged into thirty-six square mile townships. The task of mapping out the land and marking these basic grid lines was given to a special and hardy type of pioneer, the Dominion Lands surveyor.

The first surveyors to reach Central Alberta arrived in the late spring of 1880. Their task was to delineate the Fifth Initial Meridian (the 114° of longitude), which runs some eight kilometres west of the Red Deer Crossing. The leader of the group, Montague Aldous, was greatly impressed by the outstanding fertility of the Central Alber-

Before the era of roads and railroads, travel literally meant a great deal of back-breaking effort.

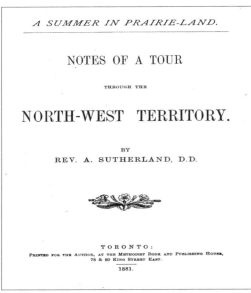

A SUMMER IN PRAIRIE-LAND.

NOTES OF A TOUR

THROUGH THE

NORTH-WEST TERRITORY.

BY

REV. A. SUTHERLAND, D.D.

TORONTO:
PRINTED FOR THE AUTHOR, AT THE METHODIST BOOK AND PUBLISHING HOUSE,
78 & 80 KING STREET EAST.
1881.

LEFT: The hardy surveyors were often said to be the last men to see Canada first because they generally preceded the arrival of the first settlers.

RIGHT: The frontispiece of *A Summer In Prairieland.* The book documented the explorations of Western Canada by a group of prominent Ontario Methodists and preceded the purchase of 180 square miles of land around Red Deer by the Saskatchewan Land and Homestead Company.

tan parkland and by the Red Deer River. He even predicted that steamboats would soon travel up the river as far as the Crossing, an occurrence which was never to take place. Nevertheless, Aldous's reports were widely circulated by the federal authorities and helped to publicize the possibilities of the area.

The late summer of 1880 saw the passage through Central Alberta of a party of prominent Methodists led by Reverend Alexander Sutherland, the secretary of the Methodist Missionary Society. Because they were on an inspection tour of the western missions, the group spent only a very brief time in the Red Deer area. Reverend Sutherland and his colleagues were still greatly impressed by the outstanding fertility and settlement opportunities of the region.

Upon his return to Ontario, Reverend Sutherland wrote a book entitled *A Summer in Prairie-Land,* which chronicled the expedition and extolled the virtues of this great new land. He also proposed that the Methodist Church should actively promote the settlement of Ontario and British Methodists in Western Canada.

Reverend Sutherland did not limit his efforts to merely writing a book. In December 1881 the Canadian government had developed a plan under which colonization companies could buy blocks of land for $2 per acre, provided that they placed at least two bona fide settlers on each square mile of land. Reverent Sutherland joined with a group of prominent Ontario Methodist businessmen and clergymen to form such a land and colonization company. Their aim was to promote Methodist settlement and to take advantage of the investment opportunities in the developing West.

Named the Saskatchewan Land and Homestead Company, it applied in early March 1882 to the government for more than 200,000 acres of land in three large blocks across the prairies. Not surprisingly, one of these blocks was centred on the Red Deer Crossing and consisted of some 180 sections of land. Originally, the company was to be granted all the sections in the Red Deer tract. However, this was later amended to only the odd numbered sections in ten townships, the even numbered sections being reserved for homesteads.

In the summer of 1882, John T. Moore, a chartered accountant from Toronto and the new managing director of the Saskatchewan Land and Homestead Company, made a trip to Western Canada to inspect the lands for which application had been made. He travelled to the Red Deer region and camped along Waskasoo Creek in what is now Rotary Picnic Park. The next morning he rode to the top of Piper's Mountain. He was so impressed by what he saw in the valley below that he became convinced that the company had made the right choice. By late September the necessary legal agreements were signed with the government.

While the Saskatchewan Land and Homestead Company was busy becoming the largest landholder in Central Alberta, the first true settlers began arriving at the Crossing. The first was Henry Meyer, who arrived in late May 1882 with a small ferry scow provided by the territorial government. The scow proved inadequate and Meyer turned his attention to building a house for himself. Misfortune struck again when he lost all the his money in a haystack fire. By late fall he transferred his claim to W.F. Bredin.

Meanwhile, Addison McPherson realized that the construction of the CPR was ending his business opportunities on the old Winnipeg–Edmonton Trail. Together with a fellow freighter named Robert W. McClellan, he embarked on an expedition through the Battle, Bow and Red Deer river valleys. As one might expect, the two men decided to settle on the same site where McPherson had built his little shack a decade before.

McClellan returned to the Crossing on July 9, 1882, and built a small house on the east side of the trail near the ford. McPherson, on the other hand, had pressing business elsewhere with his freighting outfits. He hired his brother-in-law, Burnam (Bonhomme) McGillis, to build a log house and stable to the east of McClellan's improvements. Although McPherson later wrote that he lived in his new home continuously from September 1882 to mid-1883, he actually only stayed there intermittently. It was his wife and brother-in-law who were in residence most of the time.

A handful of other settlers soon followed. In August Jack Little, a former telegraph operator from Battleford, arrived with a band of sixty-odd horses. He became the first person to settle on what is now the City of Red Deer and built a small shack just west of the mouth of Waskasoo Creek. Bad luck dogged Little, and he suffered heavy losses from severe weather, inadequate feed and disease among his animals. He was forced to abandon his claim in the summer of 1883, and he died four years later at the age of thirty-four.

Three bachelors—William Kemp, George Beatty and Jim Beatty—arrived at the Crossing in late September and awoke the

John T. Moore was the managing director of the Saskatchewan Land and Homestead Company. After an inspection trip to the Red Deer district in 1882, he recommended that the company purchase an extensive tract of land in the area.

Robert and Sarah McClellan were among the very first settlers at the Red Deer Crossing. Their stopping house was converted into Fort Normandeau in 1885.

The remarkable McKenzie family on their farm just east of Red Deer in 1887. They established one of the district's earliest sawmills and ferries. Later they built the first traffic bridge across the Red Deer River.

next morning to find half a meter of snow on the ground. Undaunted, they built a small poplar pole and sod-roofed shack, which they dubbed Sad Hollow Cabin, on a spot three kilometres upstream from the Crossing. Jim Beatty commenced the first breaking in Central Alberta that fall. By spring these men had over twenty-five acres in crop. The Beattys and Kemp were excellent craftsmen with broadaxes and helped to build many of the first log buildings in the area.

A group of Métis settlers from Headingly, Manitoba, also arrived in late September 1882 and settled along the Red Deer River between the mouths of Waskasoo Creek and Blindman River. These were hardy and ingenious settlers who built sturdy little homes. One family, the McKenzies, started the first sawmill in the area in August 1883.

The little settlement at the Crossing continued to grow throughout 1883. A small store was constructed by G.C. King of Calgary. M.P. Collins built a small stopping house, or hotel, for the freighters and travellers using the Crossing. Gradually, a river-lot settlement developed with some thirty settlers in a band fifteen kilometres upstream and another twenty kilometres downstream from the Crossing.

The traffic on the Calgary–Edmonton

Trail took a huge leap in the fall of 1883 following the arrival in Calgary of the Canadian Pacific Railroad. Freight which had formerly travelled overland from points east was now transported to Calgary by rail for shipment to Central and Northern Alberta.

The Red Deer Crossing became a key point as the traffic increased. Freighters found it convenient during particularly busy times to haul their loads as far as Red Deer and leave them there until the rush was over. Thus the Crossing became a sort of crude warehousing centre on the Calgary–Edmonton Trail.

Shortly before the railroad arrived in Calgary, regular stagecoach service started between the community and Edmonton via the Red Deer Crossing. The mode of conveyance was not elaborate. Initially, it was merely a freighter's wagon with extra seats for passengers. The cost of service was expensive, at least in terms of the value of money in the 1880s. A one-way fare was $25, return traffic being so infrequent as to make a round trip quotation unnecessary. Passengers were allowed 45 kilograms of baggage, and express freight was shipped for a little over 20 cents per kilogram.

With the settlement developing at the Crossing and the traffic on the Calgary–Edmonton Trail beginning to surge, the fed-

eral government belatedly dispatched surveyors to Central Alberta to continue the work started in 1880 by Montague Aldous. A party led by Thomas Kains of St. Thomas, Ontario, arrived in the summer of 1883 to survey the baselines and some lateral township lines. The work was hampered at times by heavy fogs and smoke, and by hard frosts on July 26 and 27. A group led by M.J. Charbonneau arrived in December 1883 to survey the section lines, work which was made easier by the incredibly mild winter of 1883–1884.

The fact that the government surveyors were completing the land division work a year and a half to two years after permanent settlement had begun was to cause great problems for the local residents. Claims had originally been laid out in a river-lot fashion similar to the system used in Manitoba's Red River valley. Charbonneau noted these river lots in his surveys, but the government chose to enforce the standard quarter-section system, probably because the Colonization Company had purchased its lands on that basis.

When the first settlers arrived they had no means of determining which land belonged to the Colonization Company even if they knew of the company's existence. Some, such as Robert McClellan, discovered that they

ROYAL MAIL LINE

LEESON & SCOTT, Proprietors.

QU'APPELLE & CALGARY, N.W.T.

Stages leave Qu'Appelle Station every Wednesday morning for Prince Albert, Battleford and Fort Pitt.

They leave Calgary every alternate Friday morning, from the 20th March, for Edmonton and Fort Saskatchewan.

Returning from Fort Pitt route every Wednesday morning, and from Edmonton every alternate Friday morning.

For particulars apply to

LEESON & SCOTT, Qu'Appelle and Calgary.

had settled on Saskatchewan Land and Homestead Company property and were forced to relocate to a neighbouring quarter. Others were so angered by the discovery that they would have to buy the land they thought they could homestead that they left the district in disgust, never to return.

The most prolonged dispute arose over the claim of Sage Bannerman, who arrived in March 1884 and started a ferry operation. Bannerman had purchased McPherson's claim for $300 and contended that he thereby acquired valid squatters rights, which superseded those of the Colonization

ABOVE: The Leeson and Scott stagecoach provided expensive but uncomfortable travel from Calgary to Edmonton. Round-trip fares were rarely quoted, as few people were interested in return passage.

BELOW: Advertisement for the Leeson and Scott stagecoach, grandly named the Royal Mail Line.

Plan of the Town of
Deerford, an
unimaginative and
never-realized townsite
designed by the
unpopular Saskatchewan
Land and Homestead
Company.

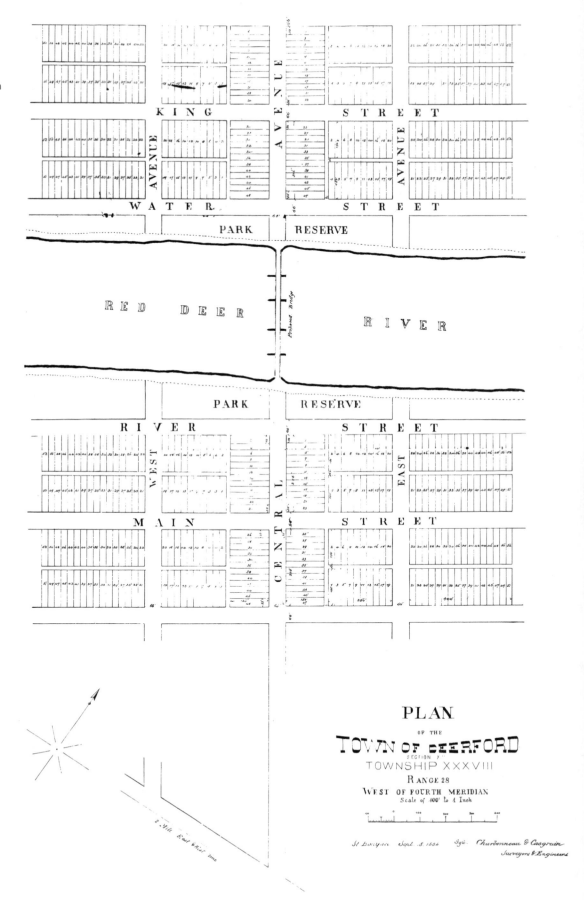

Company. The dispute raged for four years. It was only settled in 1888 when the federal government finally recognized Bannerman's claim and granted him a portion of the quarter section.

Matters generally proceeded very poorly for the Saskatchewan Land and Homestead Company. It advertised the region in such publications as *The Settlers' Pocket Guide To Homesteads In The Canadian North West.* John T. Moore made a promotional tour of Great Britain in the spring of 1884. However, the rush of new settlers to Western Canada did not match expectations. With poor land sales, the company quickly found itself in financial distress. In Central Alberta the company could not legitimately claim to have settled more than one or two of the local settlers. It hired M.J. Charbonneau and a fellow surveyor named Casgrain to survey a townsite called Deerford at the Crossing. However, the continuing dispute with Bannerman and a preoccupation with the other settlements in Saskatchewan kept the company from proceeding with the development of this townsite.

One company action did result in a lasting and profound benefit to the Red Deer area. In the fall of 1883 Moore approached one of the company's directors, Leonard Gaetz, about the possibility of settling in the Red Deer tract. Gaetz had enjoyed a distinguished career as a Methodist clergyman in his native Nova Scotia and later in Central Canada. However, he had developed health problems and was contemplating retirement from the ministry. It therefore took very little to convince him to make a trip to Central Alberta.

Gaetz was deeply impressed by the fertility and potential of the land he saw. He consequently sold his small farm near Hamilton, Ontario, and moved in April 1884 with his pregnant wife and ten children to their new Red Deer home.

The land Gaetz chose for his farm was the same flat that Jack Little had claimed for his ill-fated horse ranch two years before. It was a fortuitous choice. This was some of the very best land in the entire region. Gaetz, with his excellent skills as a farmer, soon turned his claim into a model farmstead. Moreover, since he was both an outstanding orator and gifted writer, he quickly became an effective promoter of the Red Deer area.

The Colonization Company recognized Gaetz's many talents and appointed him to the position of local agent. As a consequence of the company's agreement with the federal government, Gaetz became the local Dominion Lands agent as well.

In August 1884 G.C. King sold his little store at the Crossing to Gaetz, the operation of which was entrusted to Gaetz's eldest son, Raymond. In December the government designated the store as the local post office and named Leonard Gaetz as the first postmaster. Actually, it was Raymond who carried out the required duties.

Raymond was only eighteen years old at the time. His first experiences as a storekeeper and trader with the local Indians demonstrated his youthful inexperience. Fortunately, the new owners of the Collins stopping house, Thomas and Mary Lennie, undertook to teach the young man the fundamentals of the trade, lessons which he quickly and gratefully learned.

The situation of the Indians with whom Raymond traded was poor, and with each passing month their plight deepened. The last buffalo to be seen in the region were spotted in the summer of 1884 ten kilometres north of the Crossing. There were a mere six animals in the herd. Government rations were often inadequate, unreliable and generally unavailable to those living off the reserves.

The disappearance of the buffalo meant a drastic change of lifestyle for the Métis as well, although freighting provided them with an alternate means of making a living.

The remarkable Leonard Gaetz settled on the current site of downtown Red Deer in 1884. He became an energetic and effective promoter of Red Deer and its opportunities.

The Alberta Field Force's trip up the Calgary–Edmonton Trail in the early spring of 1885 was an often nightmarish struggle through quagmires of mud. The crossing of the Red Deer River was a near disaster when their raft was swept away by floodwaters.

The growing flood of settlers brought back the memories of their displacement from Manitoba in the early 1870s and renewed their fears for the future.

Desperation and fear soon turned to anger. In late March 1885 a large encampment of bitter natives began to form on the flat north of the Crossing. One afternoon a dozen armed and hostile tribesmen rode up to the Gaetz farmhouse and demanded to be fed. Instead of leaving their weapons in the corner, they held them at the table while they ate. Although no actual violence broke out, the family was badly frightened.

On March 26, 1885, at Duck Lake in Saskatchewan, a bloody battle was fought between a band of Métis led by Louis Riel and a group of Mounted Police and settlers. The civil war known as the Riel Rebellion had broken out in Western Canada.

The Red Deer area was spared any outbreaks of violence during the Riel Rebellion. Virtually all of the fighting took place in Saskatchewan and Northeastern Alberta.

Still, the spring of 1885 was one of the most dramatic periods in the community's history.

On April 7 a messenger named John Mowat rode from Edmonton to Calgary to plead for military assistance, making the trip in an astonishing thirty-six hours. He raised the alarm with the various settlers and freighters he met along the way. On April 8 virtually all the residents of the Red Deer area fled for the safety of Calgary. The exceptions were Bonhomme McGillis, who stayed behind to guard a cache of freight left by his brother-in-law, Addison McPherson, and William Richards, an elderly homesteader who lived several kilometres south of the Crossing.

Meanwhile, the federal government authorized the recruitment of four troops of volunteers and militia in Southern Alberta. Known as the Alberta Field Force, it was commanded by a retired and eccentric British officer, Major-General Thomas Bland Strange. The Field Force was joined in mid-April by three battalions of militia

from Eastern Canada, the 65th Mount Royal Rifles, the 92nd Winnipeg Light Infantry and the 9th Regiment de Quebec Voltigeurs.

On April 15 a party of fifteen scouts under the command of Lieutenant Coryell left Calgary for the Crossing. As they left, a heavy spring snowstorm struck, leaving nearly half a meter of wet snow on the ground. The ill-prepared scouts broke into the Gaetz store to obtain more supplies, a "looting" which some later mistakenly blamed on Indian insurgents.

On April 20 the first column of the Field Force left Calgary in a procession nearly three kilometres long. Travel was extremely arduous because the storm had left the trail in very poor shape. Still the troops made it to the Crossing in four days and crossed the river without difficulty.

On April 23 a second column under the command of Inspector Perry left Calgary. It consisted of two hundred soldiers, two dozen police, sixty-eight teamsters and a nine-pound field gun. The melting snow had turned the trail into a morass of mud, and upon arriving at the Crossing the column found the river to be in high flood. The Bannerman ferry had been broken up in the ice, so a new raft had to be built. For a while it served well in the raging stream

until the attempt was made to ferry the field gun. The cable rope snapped and the raft careened downstream with Inspector Perry and Constable W.E. Diamond vainly trying to regain control. Finally, the raft lodged against a steep bank six kilometres downstream. Then the soldiers had the strenuous task of transporting the gun back to the Crossing.

The column soon resumed its progress northward, but a party of twenty men under the command of Lieutenant J.E. Bedard Normandeau was left behind to guard the Crossing. They commandeered a two-storey stopping house, built the previous year by Robert McClellan, and began construction of a fort. The log walls were strengthened with a shell of planks filled with clay, loopholes were cut in the wall of the upper storey and a palisade with three bastions was erected around the building.

The structure, named Fort Normandeau in honour of the commanding officer, was one of three fortifications built along the Calgary–Edmonton Trail during the Riel Rebellion, the others being Fort Ostell at Ponoka and Fort Ethier at Wetaskiwin. The men were paid only fifty cents a day for their labour and were transferred to Edmonton as soon as their work was done.

By June the Riel Rebellion was rapidly

LEFT: A member of the 65th Mount Royal Rifles, Lieutenant J.E. Bedard Normandeau became the commanding officer of the fort which was to bear his name.

RIGHT: Fort Normandeau was initially a fortification of Robert McClellan's stopping house, but it eventually became a more elaborate complex of buildings. After the Riel Rebellion, the fort was used as quarters for a detachment of the North West Mounted Police.

The simple log school-house, halfway between the Crossing settlement and the Leonard Gaetz farm, served not only as the district's first educational facility, but also as the community's social centre.

coming to an end. The fort was briefly occupied by the Alberta Mounted Rifles and the Crossing was heavily used by brigades of teamsters hauling supplies for the military. However, by midsummer the soldiers had left, the flow of traffic had begun to ebb and the Crossing returned to its usual peaceful state.

The Riel Rebellion and its immediate aftermath proved to be an economic bonanza to the local settlers. Some made small fortunes from freighting, while others made money from contracts with the government for the sale of supplies to the military. Those such as Leonard Gaetz, who had suffered losses, were eventually compensated by the War Claims Commission.

The claim of Robert McClellan for $1645.75 for damages to his hotel was not accepted by the Commissioners. They claimed to have no record of Inspector Perry being authorized to convert the structure into a fort. McClellan's problems proved to be short-lived, however. In the summer of

1886 a detachment of thirteen North West Mounted Police under the command of Inspector T.W. Chalmers was posted to the Red Deer Crossing. For their accommodation the government rented Fort Normandeau for the sum of $35 a month and also contracted McClellan to build officers' quarters for which an additional $10 a month rent was paid.

In the aftermath of the Rebellion the position of the Saskatchewan Land and Homestead Company continued to deteriorate. Land sales became virtually nonexistent as the flow of new settlers to the West dried up. New investors became hard to find. Both the company and the Canadian West came to be viewed as bad risks.

The company's situation was not unique, and the federal government agreed to renegotiate the various land and colonization companies' contracts. In June 1886 the indentures were cancelled, and the Saskatchewan Land and Homestead Company was reincorporated as a commercial land company

Freighters having just left Calgary on their way to the Alberta Lumber Company's new mill site on the south bank of the Red Deer River, 1888.

rather than a quasi-religious colonization company. Leonard Gaetz ceased to be the local Dominion Lands agent. Henceforth, prospective settlers had to register their claims at the lands office in Calgary.

Nothing about these new arrangements made the company any more popular with the local settlers. In 1887 a petition signed by over two dozen settlers was sent to Ottawa asking that the company's land rights north of the river be cancelled. The government did not reply until 1894 when it claimed it could no longer do anything.

The local correspondent to the *Edmonton Bulletin,* Robert McClellan, sarcastically asked in his column whether or not "the only and original, religious and secular colonization company which lords it over our most fertile lands" would do anything about providing a school. He added that perhaps "the only and original" would provide a church instead.

Both school and church development occurred in 1887, although the Land Com-

pany had virtually nothing to do with either. In early April 1887 the Presbyterian Missionary Society sent a student minister, William Neilly, to the Crossing "to found a mission school for the settlers' children and expound the Gospel to the public in general on Sabbath days." Sage Bannerman provided accommodation in what may have been McPherson's old shack near the ford. Neilly wrote to his superiors that when he arrived he had "only two coppers to rub together." He added that he still had his two cents as there was no place to spend his money.

On May 1, 1887, the first Anglican service was held by Reverend E.K. Mathieson at Fort Normandeau. The next day a meeting was held at the R.A. McKenzie house to organize a parish.

In June the local Methodist congregation, which had been led by lay minister Isaac Gaetz, asked the Conference to appoint a student minister. In July 1887 William A. Vrooman arrived to take over the charge.

One of the bunk cars used by the labourers on the construction of the Calgary–Edmonton Railroad.

During the summer of 1887 the local settlers began work on a regular school to take the place of the informal mission school run by Neilly. A log schoolhouse was built on a site midway between the Crossing settlement and the home of the large Gaetz family (just north of present-day 64th Avenue and Riverside Drive). It was a very modest structure. Unpainted and heated by a rusty box stove, it was furnished with some homemade desks as well as some benches for Sunday church services. The playground was a clearing next to the trail. Water was hauled up from the neighbouring river.

On September 12, 1887, the Red Deer Central Protestant School District No. 104 was officially formed with trustees Leonard Gaetz, John Jost Gaetz and George Wilbert Smith. William Kemp and Robert McClellan took over the latter two men's positions six weeks later. The first class had seven pupils, five Gaetzes and two McClellans. The first teacher was William Vrooman, who had been granted a provisional certificate by the Territorial Department of Education. Vrooman left the following spring and was replaced by G.W. Smith, who had a first-class teacher's certificate from Nova Scotia.

The settlement continued to grow slowly but steadily as a number of new settlers moved into the area. In the summer of 1887 work began on the area's first industrial venture, the Alberta Lumber Company. The company originally wanted to build its mill at the Crossing. However, it found the price asked by the Saskatchewan Land and Homestead Company and the legal problems with the Bannerman farm to be obstacles too great to overcome. Instead, a site was chosen a short distance below the mouths of the Little Red Deer and Medicine rivers.

The project was dogged by bad luck, and the mill was built very slowly. An attempt was made to improve its prospects by having the government place restrictive regulations on the McKenzie brothers' mill. A local outcry caused the government to temper its action. Ironically, part of the Alberta Lumber Company's mill was subsequently built with lumber sawn by the McKenzies.

The ALC's mill had been located on a site

where the proposed Alberta and Athabasca Railway Company was to cross the Red Deer River. This railroad venture failed to materialize, and the isolated location of the mill contributed to its ultimate failure.

The Alberta and Athabasca Railway Company was but one of several proposals to build a rail line from Calgary to Edmonton. Most were mere phantoms. In February 1890, however, the federal government chartered the Calgary and Edmonton Railroad Company, and in June 1890 actual construction of the line commenced.

The implications of this development for the Red Deer settlement were enormous. Rail transport was far superior to the small wagons and Red River carts currently using the Calgary–Edmonton Trail. A successful railroad venture spelled the end of the traditional freighters' business. It would also make the region much more accessible and attractive for settlement and would create wonderful new opportunities for the district. Even before the actual rail line was built through the region, there was a large increase in the number of new settlers.

Leonard Gaetz, who never lagged in his boosterism of the district, wrote a number of glowing articles for the *Calgary Herald* early in 1890. As well, in late February he journeyed to Ottawa, where he testified on the potential of Central Alberta before the Standing Committee on Agriculture and Colonization. His testimony, later printed in a pamphlet called *Report of Six Years' Experience Of A Farmer In The Red Deer District*, was circulated by the Department of Agriculture as an encouragement to settlers.

Gaetz did not limit his efforts to speeches, articles and pamphlets. He offered the railroad company an undivided half interest in his farm, Bellevue, which by this time had grown to 1,200 acres, if the railroad would cross the river on his property. The Calgary and Edmonton Railroad Company readily accepted this generous offer. In November 1890, when the rail line

had been built as far as Red Deer, the new townsite was surveyed on Gaetz's farmstead. On November 23 the first train with passengers travelled from Red Deer to Calgary in a time of just over three and one-half hours. Among those on board were the Reverend and Mrs. Gaetz and one of their daughters.

These developments struck the death knell for the old Crossing settlement, which now stood over six kilometres west of the rail line. The local residents quite naturally wanted to be as close to the railroad as possible. Once the lots in the new townsite went on sale in January 1891, people began to move to the new Red Deer. New exciting times had come to the district, and the old hamlet faded into memory as the "Old Crossing."

Chapter 4

New Times, Boom Times

LEFT: With the arrival of the railroad in 1890–91, a new townsite quickly sprang up on the former grain fields of Reverend Leonard Gaetz.

ABOVE: Leonard Gaetz on the way to his garden in the new town of Red Deer.

New times and boom times followed the arrival of the railroad in Central Alberta. The Townsite Company's agents—Osler, Hammond and Nanton—originally planned to start selling lots in the new townsite in May 1891. However, there was such a heavy demand that sales actually commenced in January. Prices ranged from $40 to $200 per lot with demand being particularly strong for corner lots priced between $100 and $125.

As the former residents of the Crossing settlement and new arrivals to the district began to buy up property in the new Red Deer, a tremendous burst of construction activity followed. In March the *Calgary Herald* reported the construction of five new stores, a hotel and a number of residences. The grandest of these new homes was the one being built by Leonard Gaetz at an estimated cost of nearly $3,000.

The building of the new railroad station provided a good indication of the pace of construction. Work was started in mid-May by a crew of twelve men. By May 30 they had started painting the new structure.

The first townsite plan of Red Deer was laid out by George Bemister in November 1890. There is no recorded reason why he set the streets east and west and the avenues north and south, when the opposite pattern was the usual. Nevertheless, the main street, Ross, was originally called an avenue.

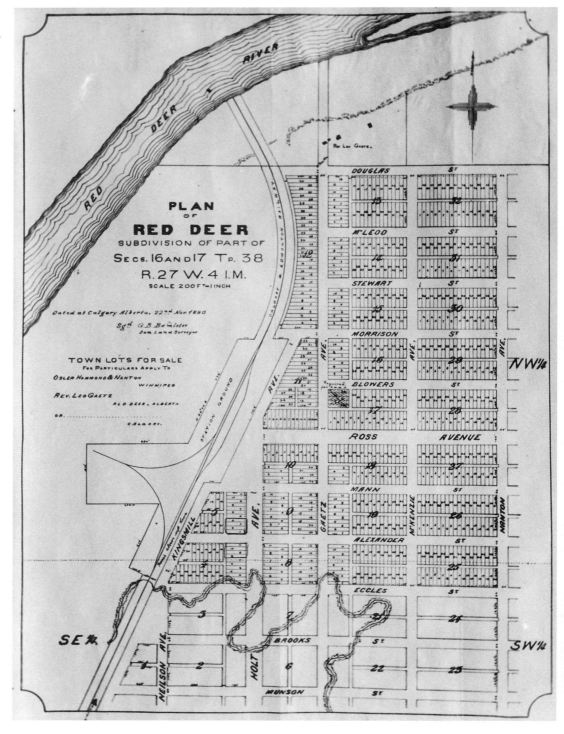

The feverish pace of activity was not limited to the new townsite. For the cash-starved local settlers, there were plenty of jobs working on the rail line north to Edmonton. Wages, at least in the terms of the 1890s, were excellent. Labourers were paid $1 a day plus board, teamsters $2.50 a day with board for themselves and their horses.

For settlers well enough established to have successfully raised some crops, there was now an excellent market for their produce. Oats sold for seventy-five to eighty cents per bushel and potatoes fetched a dollar per bushel. A heavy frost on August 10 drove prices even higher. Any produce not snapped up by the local contractors

could now be shipped south by rail to Calgary.

By midsummer the rail line had been completed as far as South Edmonton. On July 27, 1891, a train travelled the entire 310-kilometre length of the line. In mid-August the last stage coach carried the mail from Calgary to Edmonton. On August 23 the CPR took over the operation of the rail line from the Calgary and Edmonton Railroad Company. The new transportation link between Northern and Southern Alberta was now complete.

While the old trail through the Red Deer Crossing was overshadowed by its new rival, it was not completely abandoned. A number of settlers and travellers continued to use it as they found the railroad company's freight and passenger rates to be too expensive.

Because of the continuing traffic at the Old Crossing, the North West Mounted Police did not move into the townsite from Fort Normandeau until June 1893. However, the constables did not seem to have had much regard for the history of the old settlement. They used the fort's stockade for firewood during the winter of 1892–93.

With the surge of activity in Central Alberta following the arrival of the railroad, there was even some new development at the Old Crossing. In the spring of 1892 the Methodist Church began construction of an Indian industrial school on the riverbank northwest of the ford. It is an indication of the hardiness of the early pioneers that some of the settlers who worked on this project walked over twelve kilometres and waded across the Red Deer River on their way to work.

Most of the new development, however, continued to be centred in the townsite on the railroad. In 1892 several new businesses and residences were constructed. A new settler from Ontario, William Piper, recognized the potential of the clay beds along the South Hill and started one of Red

ABOVE: Reportedly the first train into Red Deer. The photo was taken by William Piper, who had come to the fledgling community to start a brickyard. Note the elk antlers on the smokestack of the train.

BELOW: The Indian Industrial School was built at the Red Deer Crossing in 1892 by the Methodist Church with federal government support. The intent was to train natives in agriculture, vocational and domestic labour in order to help assimilate them into the "whiteman's" way of life.

Ross Street, looking west toward the train station, 1893. By the mid-1890s growth in the community had slowed to a crawl. Red Deer remained a tiny hamlet nestled in the river valley.

Deer's most important early industries: a brickyard. In March 1892 work commenced on Red Deer's first church, the Methodist, and on June 26 the new structure was officially dedicated. Meanwhile, another hotel, the Alberta, was built on Ross Street near the train station.

There were also a number of developments in the social and recreational affairs of the community. On July 10, 1891, Red Deer held its first Dominion Day celebrations, which included a social and a dance in the new Wilkins Hall on Ross Street. In September 1891 the first club, the Red Deer Rifle Association, was organized with George Greene, the community's first lawyer, as secretary.

On Halloween 1891 the Red Deer Agricultural Society was formed with Leonard Gaetz as the first president. In the following year, on October 11, 1892, the first Red Deer Fair was held at the Wilkins Hall. There were extensive grain, vegetable and handicraft displays as well as livestock and commercial exhibits. Newspaper accounts referred to it as "an unqualified success."

With the shift of the settlement, the school board decided to move the school from the log building which stood midway between the Old Crossing and the new townsite. In March 1893 the board passed a

bylaw authorizing the rental of the second floor of the Burch store on the northeast corner of Gaetz Avenue and Ross Street. The old schoolhouse was sold to the Horn Hill school board for $100, and it was subsequently relocated to that district.

The early 1890s were very dry years and the district was plagued by a number of very bad prairie fires. In the spring of 1892 an immense series of blazes blackened the 200-kilometre stretch between the Bow and the Red Deer rivers. Only the strenuous efforts of the entire population of Red Deer saved the hamlet from destruction. In October workmen saved the nearly completed Indian Industrial School from being destroyed by another blaze.

The early 1890s also were years of economic depression. Although the construction of the railroad had given the district a two year boost, by 1893 Central Alberta had fallen into the economic doldrums. The pace of development slowed to a crawl. The unfortunate Saskatchewan Land and Homestead Company held a large land sale in Calgary on October 17, 1893, but there were very few buyers.

One of the notable victims of the economic hard times was Red Deer's first newspaper which was started in March 1894 by D.H. Murphy. It had been hoped that this

four-page weekly would become a vigorous promoter of the district. Instead, the paper was beset by financial difficulties almost immediately and ceased publication by the end of April.

Despite the problems and the hardships, there were still several important developments in the community. Red Deer's first board of trade was formed in March 1894, and one of its first actions was an attempt to save the newspaper.

Another initiative met with better success. The board undertook to have the hamlet formally organized. On June 15, 1894, a form of municipal government was established under the Unincorporated Towns Ordinance. R.M. Pardue was elected as the first overseer and the tax rate was set at two mills. The following year the territorial government passed the Village Ordinance, and Red Deer became a village instead of an unincorporated town.

Meanwhile, the school board decided to build a brick schoolhouse on a site on Nanton (48th) Avenue, which had been purchased from the Townsite Company for $250. Although the structure had only two rooms, it was two storeys in height, as a tall, narrow building was thought to be easier to heat. With only two dozen pupils on the register in 1894, the upper classroom was

not immediately needed. It was consequently rented for a number of club meetings and public gatherings as well as court sessions.

In November 1893 the territorial government contracted David McKenzie to build a traffic bridge across the river on the north end of Gaetz Avenue. Although neither David McKenzie nor his brother Roderick had any training as bridge builders, these ingenious and capable men still managed to erect a structure which was to survive ice floes and floods for five years. Their accom-

ABOVE: By the late 1890s the economic fortunes of Red Deer had begun to improve. By 1898 it had become a bustling little community again.

BELOW: In 1894 the Red Deer Public School District built a two-storey brick schoolhouse fronting on Nanton (48th) Avenue. Although not very well built, it remained in use until 1928.

Red Deer's first traffic bridge was erected in 1894 by the McKenzie brothers, resourceful men who lacked any formal bridge-building training. Nevertheless, the bridge lasted until the floods of 1899.

plishment also dealt one final blow to the Old Crossing as there was now a year-round and safe way to cross the river.

Although Red Deer developed into a small quiet village, there were occasional incidents which shattered the peace of the community. On one occasion in 1892 a fugitive murderer named Ole Mickelson was spotted north of Red Deer as he was attempting to flee the district. A civilian posse was hastily formed and pursued the outlaw to the Wilkins' ranch on the north bank of the river. A gun battle ensued and Mickelson made a frantic dash for the farmhouse. Fearing for the safety of Mrs. Wilkins and her daughter, one of the posse, William Bell, brought the fugitive down with a shot from his rifle. The authorities subsequently laid a charge of manslaughter against Bell, but it was dismissed by the jury after a highly publicized and controversial trial.

In 1893 the school board dismissed the popular local school teacher, Miss Margaret Duncan, after a complaint from a prominent resident. A public indignation meeting was held, and the complainant was burned in effigy. The secretary-treasurer of the school board feared further acts of retribution (i.e. that he would be the next one to be burned in effigy). He wrote to the federal authorities demanding strong action by the police before "blood was shed" and "many lives lost." No such outbreaks took place, and the issue slowly faded away after a spate of angry letters and a lawsuit.

A year later the village overseer became involved in an ill-conceived obscene prank on a woman who operated a local hotel. Her husband became extremely indignant, and after tracking down the culprit, he proceeded to horsewhip the man on the street. The injured man attempted to have a charge of attempted murder laid, but the police refused to act, possibly because the assailant was a former constable. A stormy public protest meeting was held. The police inspector in charge of the division travelled down from Edmonton to investigate. Charges of assault causing bodily harm were eventually laid, but a panel of three justices of the peace acquitted the hotelman.

By the late 1890s economic prosperity had started to return to the community. In 1897 a 15,000-bushel grain elevator was built by the Dominion Elevator Company. The creamery, which had been built in 1894, was reopened with the assistance of a government leasing agreement with the new owner, A.H. Trimble.

The improved economic prospects were fuelled by an improved Canadian economy, better prices for agricultural produce and the opening of new markets, particularly in the Kootenay region of British Columbia, which was experiencing a mining and lumbering boom. The importance of these new B.C. markets is evident in the fact that of the 8,500 kilograms of butter produced by the Red Deer Creamery in 1897, nearly 7,000 kilograms were shipped to the Kootenays.

Even the climate began to change. The wet cycle returned and the region turned green and lush with the substantial increase in rainfall. Depressions turned into lakes, and creeks and rivers swelled.

New settlers began to pour into the region at a phenomenal rate. In 1896–97 the Red Deer land office recorded a mere twenty-one homestead entries. In 1898 this figure jumped to over 100. In 1899 it more than tripled, and in 1900 the number of entries doubled again to over 700. In the words of J.G. Jessup, the Dominion Lands Agent, Red Deer had "caught the favouring breeze." He reported that "the streets are lined with wagons loaded with grain and farm produce, merchants have doubled and tripled their staffs, fresh representatives of the different trades are coming in, and the Calgary and Edmonton Railway company has been obliged to enlarge their general traffic service in order to meet the growing demand." New times and boom times had returned once again to Central Alberta.

This growth and prosperity was reflected in the social, religious and recreational life of the community. In 1898 the Presbyterians constructed Red Deer's second church with the Reverend Dr. McQueen of Edmonton conducting the inaugural services on July 3. The Red Deer Board of Trade, dormant since May 1895, was revived in March 1899

at a meeting held in the sample rooms of the Alberta Hotel. In the same month the Northwest Entomological Society was formed, the first of a number of strong natural history organizations which have been active throughout the Red Deer area.

The Masonic Lodge, which had folded after two years of existence in 1896, was officially reinstituted in 1899. On September 4 it assisted with the laying of the cornerstone of St. Luke's Anglican Church. This impressive structure on the corner of Gaetz Avenue and McLeod (54th) Street was built with sandstone from a newly opened quarry on the south bank of the Red Deer River, a short distance upstream from the village.

ABOVE: St. Luke's Anglican Church was an impressive new sandstone edifice started in 1899. Because of ongoing shortages of funds, the parishioners were forced to build the church in sections over a period of seven years.

BELOW: The Reinholt Quarry was opened on the south bank of the Red Deer River in the late 1890s. It supplied sandstone for several impressive new buildings in the rapidly growing community.

The disappearance in 1899 of Maude Waldbrooke, the matron of the Indian Industrial School, remains one of Red Deer's most enduring mysteries.

Competitive team sports started in 1897 with the first being cricket, baseball and football (soccer). Lawn tennis was first played the following year. In December 1898 an outdoor skating rink opened on Morrison (52nd) Street. Curling games, which had previously been held on the ice of the river, were first played at the new rink on Boxing Day. Hockey games soon followed.

The late 1890s also saw a number of new services started in the village. In December 1897 Red Deer's first restaurant opened on Ross Street, and a year and one-half later, two dress-making shops opened for business. The fall of 1899 saw the construction of Red Deer's first Chinese laundry, a welcome development for the bachelors of the community.

Despite the boom and general good times, there were still many hardships and setbacks. The wet weather turned roads into quagmires. Outbreaks of "swamp fever," or glanders, caused widespread losses of horses. In August 1899 torrential rains caused a severe shortage of building material when the brickyard's supply of brick clay was washed away, the road to the stone quarry became impassable and flooding along the river swept away the local sawmill's supply of logs. The river flood also severely damaged the traffic bridge, and the following

spring the whole structure was destroyed when the ice went out. The territorial government spent $15,000 to construct a new steel bridge. However, the piers were very poorly built, and the spans were swept away during the next spring breakup. Temporary arrangements were made to plank the railway bridge, and a watchman was hired to control the traffic until the new traffic bridge was finished in the spring of 1902.

One of Red Deer's most enduring mysteries occurred in August 1899. The new matron of the Indian Industrial School, Maud Lillian Waldbrooke, suddenly vanished, in the words of the *Calgary Herald,* "as completely as if the earth had opened and swallowed her up." Widespread searches were conducted. As it was feared that she may have accidentally fallen into the river and drowned, the stream was dragged by the police. However, all these efforts proved fruitless.

Shortly thereafter a number of strange and frightening events took place at the school. The farm instructor, agitated over the disappearance of Miss Waldbrooke, fired at a stranger who was lurking near his home. Although it was thought that the unidentified man had been wounded, no trace of him was later found. The school principal's house was ransacked, but nothing was stolen. The school's piggery was destroyed by arson and a few days later, the farm instructor and some pupils surprised a man who had broken into the stable. The man fired shots at them as he fled. Still later, the school watchman was shot at by an unseen assailant.

These incidents eventually came to an end. While a reward of $1,000 was offered to anyone who could locate Miss Waldbrooke, she was never seen or heard from again. It remains a mystery to this day whether she was a victim of murder or misadventure.

Despite the various adversities and tragedies, the era of growth and prosperity continued, and faith in the future remained

PRESENTED WITH THE COMPLIMENTS OF

BRUMPTON & GAETZ

THE RED DEER MERCHANTS.

R.L.GAETZ. MAYOR

D.S.LONG
FIRST MAYOR

W.A.MOORE
AND COUNCIL

R.C.BRUMPTON

Wᵐ SPRINGBETT

F.E.WILKINS

L.C.FULMER SEC.TREAS.

H.SHARPLES

G.W.GREENE SOLICITOR

RED DEER INCORPORATED 20ᵀᴴ JUNE 1901

On June 20, 1901, Red Deer was incorporated as a town with an official population of 323. Issues for the first council included roaming livestock, unauthorized manure dumps and a dead horse in the middle of Ross Street.

undaunted. Although Red Deer was smaller than the other villages in the region, such as Lacombe and Innisfail, moves were made to have Red Deer incorporated as a town. At the village annual meeting in December 1900, a committee was formed to investigate the issue. In April a recommendation to proceed was ratified by the ratepayers by a vote of seventeen to four. The territorial government had no major objections to the application for incorporation. On June 20, 1901, Red Deer was officially designated as a town.

Elections for the first mayor and council were set for July 4. Under the provisions of the town charter, those eligible to vote were men, unmarried women and widows twenty-one years of age or older who assessed property worth at least $200. All married women, regardless of wealth, were ineligible to vote. The seven town councillors were all elected by acclamation. There was, however, a close contest for the position of mayor with Raymond Gaetz defeating his oppo-

nent, William Postill, by a margin of only one vote.

The new mayor and council tackled their responsibilities with such great enthusiasm that it took six sessions over a period of three weeks to complete the inaugural meeting. Council approved a budget of $2592.15, an amount triple that spent by the village in the previous year. In keeping with Red Deer's sense of pride and accomplishment, council adopted as the town motto *Ex elegantia pabulum.*

Some of the first issues faced by town council reflected the small size of the community. Bylaws were passed to prevent livestock from roaming the streets. Subsequently the new poundkeeper rounded up forty cows and calves on one Saturday night, and two days later he impounded seventy head of sheep. Council also received complaints about loads of manure being dumped into a coulee east of McKenzie (49th) Avenue, and it ordered one resident to remove the decayed remains of a horse from the east

The Red Deer Butter and Cheese Manufacturing Association was a local venture which sought to build a new industry based on the dairying in the district.

end of Ross Street. Arrangements were later made to establish a town dump west of the railroad tracks.

In the spring of 1902 the town began to acquire the block south of Ross Street between McKenzie and Nanton Avenue for a civic square. Part of the impressive sandstone Greene Block on the southwest corner of Gaetz Avenue and Ross Street had been rented as a town council chamber. However, in April 1903 council meetings were moved to the parlour of the old Postill house on the Town Square. Two police cells were installed in the kitchen, and an old frame stable was attached to the house to accommodate the town's fire equipment. Although rudimentary in appearance, Red Deer now had a town hall.

In the period following Red Deer's incorporation as a town, the community continued to enjoy spectacular growth. From a mere 320 residents in the spring of 1901, the population jumped to 850 in the following year. Settlers continued to pour into the surrounding area as well. In 1903 the land titles office recorded nearly 1,500 entries for homesteads.

The physical appearance of the community underwent a dramatic change. Dozens of new houses were built. Substantial new business blocks were constructed along Ross Street, Gaetz Avenue and adjoining thoroughfares. Many of these new buildings were built of brick, partly because of new fire control regulations established by the town.

With the growing demand for brick, a second brickyard was opened in 1902 by the Red Deer Brick and Lumber Company. This new enterprise was on the same roadway as the Piper's brickyard with the consequence that Victoria Avenue (43rd Street) was then known as Brick Street.

Among the notable commercial buildings constructed at that time were the *Red Deer Echo* newspaper office (1901), the Alexandra Hotel (1902), the Purdy Opera House (1903) and the H.H. Gaetz Block (1903), which included both a drugstore and a new post office. In keeping with Red Deer's economic status as an agricultural service centre, a new creamery was built by the Red Deer Butter and Cheese Manufacturing Association. A number of farm implement warehouses, another grain elevator and a flour mill were built as well.

There were also substantial developments with respect to Red Deer's public buildings. In 1902 the school board found that the schoolhouse could no longer accommodate the growing number of students. A new two-room, two-storey addition was constructed at a cost of $3,000. A third teacher was hired and appointed principal of the expanded school at a salary of $55 per month. In 1903 the school board decided there was sufficient demand to add a high school department with classes being conducted in the fourth room of the schoolhouse.

In early 1901 the community decided to build a hospital as a memorial tribute to Angus Jenkins, Archibald McNichol and Charles Cruickshanks, three local young men who had served with the Lord Strathcona Horse and had given their lives during the South African (Boer) War (1899–1902). A public fund-raising campaign was commenced with Lord Strathcona, patron of the regiment, donating $1,000 and the Victorian Order of Nurses contributing $2,000, building plans and a great deal of other assistance. Construction began in the spring of 1903 on the hill on the southwest edge of town, and by April 1904 the thirteen-bed facility was ready for occupancy. The first patient, W.N. Snider, was admitted with typhoid fever, but unfortunately, he suffered a relapse and passed away a few weeks later. Drs. Howard and Henrietta Denovan performed the first surgical operation on April 25, and on May 3 the hospital board established a schedule of fees for the use of the operating room.

In 1903 the federal government let a contract for the construction of a court house on the block immediately west of the civic square. This structure was to include accommodations for the Dominion Lands and Customs and Excise offices. Work was very slow in getting started and the basement was not excavated until May 1904. The federal employees were not able to move into their new quarters until March 1906.

The early turn of the century brought a number of important advances in the realm of utilities and public services. In December 1902 a group of local businessmen headed by John T. Moore incorporated the Western Telephone Company. A few months later they were granted a twenty-five year franchise by the town council. The company was slow in getting started, and the town actually got long-distance telephone service first when the Bell Telephone Company built a phone line from Calgary to Edmonton with connections to Red Deer.

Early in 1904 the Bell Company decided to provide local telephone service. Businesses were charged $30 per year and householders were charged $21 per annum. By March 1904 Bell had nearly forty subscribers. Meanwhile, Moore and his associates reorganized their telephone and electrical interests into the Western General Electric Company. By the end of October 1904 the Western General was able to provide the

first electricity to the town. The company also installed the first central-energy telephone system in Alberta, and in January 1905 it commenced local telephone service.

Not surprisingly there was strong rivalry between the Western General and the Bell Telephone Company for the community's business. Moreover, after John T. Moore's election as Red Deer's first MLA in 1905, he became a strong proponent of a government-owned telephone system to compete with Bell on a province-wide basis. Eventually, the Western General, with its technologically superior equipment and its rates of only $25 per year for businesses and $10 per year for homes, triumphed over its giant competitor. By 1907 the number of Bell's

ABOVE: In the early 1900s Red Deer began to blossom into a substantial-looking community with numerous new brick and sandstone business blocks in the downtown area.

BELOW: Many of the workmen at the Piper's Brickyard were recent immigrants from Scandinavia and the United States.

RIGHT: Piper's Brickyard in 1901, looking east from the Hospital Hill toward what is now Parkvale. After the turn of the century there was so much construction in Red Deer that a second brickyard opened on the west end of Brick (43rd) Street.

BELOW: A welcome addition to the community of Red Deer was the opening of the thirteen-bed Memorial Hospital in April 1904. Unfortunately, one of the first two patients died shortly thereafter from typhoid fever.

subscribers had dwindled to fewer than a dozen. In May 1908 Alberta Government Telephones bought out Bell's Alberta operations, including Red Deer's long-distance exchange. The Western General now had the local market to itself and raised its rates an additional $5 per year for business and an extra $13 per year for homeowners.

In 1904 town council took steps to have a waterworks system installed. An agreement was struck with the Western General Electric to provide the necessary electrical power. On Halloween 1904 Mayor Edward Michener assisted with the installation of the first section of pipe on the corner of Gaetz Avenue and Douglas (55th) Street. On April

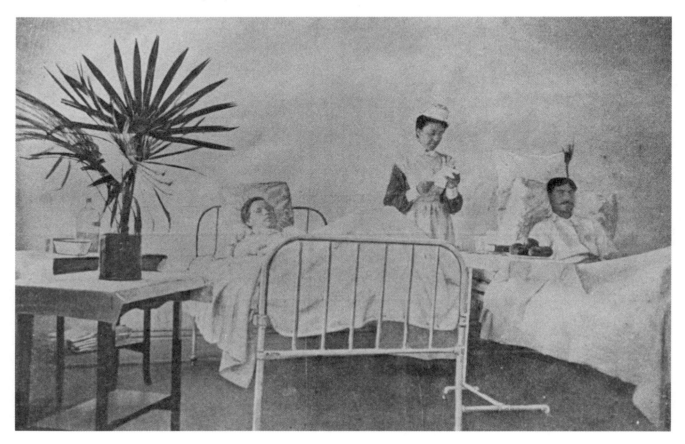

In 1904 Red Deer town council began to install the community's first waterworks system. As this crew working along Alexander (48th) Street shows, it was a labour-intensive project.

25, 1905, the system became operational, and Red Deer now had running water. A sewer system, however, was not to follow until late in 1907, and then only after a considerable amount of public controversy.

The year 1904 was bad for fires. A blaze in April destroyed a livery barn and a residence. Despite the loss, the local ratepayers rejected the purchase of a new fire engine by a narrow margin of thirty-five votes to thirty-four. In mid-September another blaze destroyed the Michener Block with the loss being estimated at $22,000. Within a week of this second disaster, town council authorized the formation of a sixteen-man volunteer fire brigade with the firemen being paid thirty-five cents per hour and the fire chief receiving fifty cents per hour. Horace Meeres, the first fire chief, was also given use of all but the parlour of the Town Hall (Postill house) as living quarters. In 1906 a substantial two-storey brick building, optimistically named Fire Hall No. 1, was built on the civic square. The town council chamber was moved to this building shortly thereafter.

In December 1903 an covered ice-skating curling rink was built, which provided a great boost to the winter sports activities in the community. The following winter women's hockey got under way with the first games

being charitable events in aid of the new Memorial Hospital. The senior team was dubbed the "Stars" while the younger women played for a team called the "Skookems." Occasionally, the two teams would combine to play a men's team, with the men being required to play with only one hand during the contests.

In 1902 the Red Deer Fair moved from its former site at the CPR roundhouse to a new site near Waskasoo Creek on the southeast side of the town. Two years later the Agricultural Society bought an additional two acres and had a race track laid out. It also optimistically built a grandstand capable of seating as many as 1,500 people and named the whole complex Alexandra Park in honour of Queen Alexandra, wife of King Edward VII.

In the spring of 1905 the Baptists built Red Deer's fourth church on the southeast corner of Blowers (51st) Street and McKenzie (49th) Avenue. In the fall of the same year, Father Henri Voisin built a small Roman Catholic Church on Alexander (48th) Street. The poor priest was forced to put the shingles on the building by himself because his volunteer helpers were too frightened to work on the steep roof.

Early in 1905 the *Red Deer News* commenced publication in competition with the

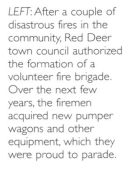

LEFT: After a couple of disastrous fires in the community, Red Deer town council authorized the formation of a volunteer fire brigade. Over the next few years, the firemen acquired new pumper wagons and other equipment, which they were proud to parade.

RIGHT: In 1905 the Roman Catholics built a frame church on Alexander (48th) Street. Because of ambitious future plans, the tiny structure was built with a substantial roof, which proved to be difficult and dangerous to shingle.

Alberta Advocate, which had been in operation since May 1903. In keeping with the strong partisan politics of the time, the *Advocate* was stalwartly Liberal while the *News* was resolutely Conservative. The first editor of the *News*, though, was George Love, a former mayor who had also served as the editor of the *Advocate* the year before.

A seamier side of Red Deer appeared about the same time when a brothel opened on the north side of town. A government inspector from Edmonton raided the establishment in June 1905, and the operator was convicted of the illegal sale of liquor, "keeping a house of ill fame and being an inmate of same." Despite the resulting $100 fine the house did not close until it was raided again in February of the following year. The magistrate who heard the case was also the editor of one of the newspapers, and he provided front page coverage of the case. He decided, however, not to print the names of the men found in the house nor did he include them in his official report.

The appearance of vice and other moral shortcomings is often considered to be the inevitable consequence of boom times. By the midpoint of the decade Red Deer was certainly continuing to experience a strong boom. The population had jumped to over 1,500. In May 1905 the local land titles office

recorded the largest percentage increase in homestead entries of any land office in the nation. Nevertheless, Red Deer remained a generally law-abiding and peaceable community. The episode with the brothel was an isolated one, and there were only a few other cases involving the illegal sale of liquor and illicit gambling.

The sense of optimism and prosperity was such, however, that when Alberta became a province in September 1905, the citizens of Red Deer made a concerted attempt to have the town designated as the new capital city. On April 17, 1906, the mayor and council invited the Lieutenant-Governor, the Premier and all the MLAs to come and view the obvious assets of the community. The dignitaries were shown the land on the brow of Michener Hill, which the town was prepared to donate as a site for the legislature building. They were then taken to the Arlington Hotel for an extravagant banquet with the entertainment and speeches lasting until 4:45 A.M. Later that morning the guests were roused for further ceremonies at the Canadian Pacific Railroad station park during which the Lieutenant-Governor and the MLAs each planted a commemorative spruce tree. Everyone professed to be greatly impressed by Red Deer and its hospitality, but when the MLAs returned to Edmon-

ton, they overwhelmingly voted to confirm that city as the capital.

The town council neglected to invite the members of the school board to the ceremonies and banquet with the provincial legislators. As a result, when the school trustees proudly opened a new eight-room public school in October 1907, they invited the Premier and several cabinet ministers, but pointedly did not invite the town councillors to the ceremonies.

The construction of the beautiful new three-storey schoolhouse, later nicknamed the Castle, reflected the tremendous growth and progress of the Red Deer Public School District. The need to rent extra classroom space in such buildings as the Orange Hall and the Purdy Opera House was now eliminated, and the old school house—with its lack of wiring, plumbing and adequate heat—was left vacant. Within three years, however, rising enrolment forced the school board to reopen the 1894 schoolhouse as a high school after the completion of some basic renovations. Later concrete buttresses were erected to keep the brick walls from falling down.

In 1908 the local Roman Catholics decided to form a separate school district. Father Voisin persuaded the Daughters of Wisdom, a congregation of teaching and nurs-

ing sisters, to come to Red Deer from Eastern Canada and France. A large brick convent named St. Joseph's was built on the brow of the North Hill. In January 1909 the separate school board arranged to rent classroom space there for $200 a year. The sisters boarded many of the students. The sisters were held in such high regard that a number of those who stayed at the convent were from Protestant families.

The same summer that St. Joseph's convent was built, the Fathers of St. Mary of Tinchebray built a three-storey brick presbytery a short distance to the west. Six years later they built St. Mary's Apostolic School north of their residence. In 1909 a new Roman Catholic Church was constructed southwest of the convent. Initially called Sacred Heart and later renamed Our Lady of Sorrows, this church consisted of a large concrete basement covered by a wooden peaked roof.

The Roman Catholic mission on the hill overlooked a growing settlement on the north side of the river. In 1905 a large-scale sawmill was built by G.H. Bawtinheimer on the west side of the CPR tracks. The following year the Great West Lumber Company bought the operation and expanded it. As many as 100 men were employed by the lumber company, and it is not surprising

The view of Red Deer as seen from the proposed site for the provincial legislature building. In 1905 Red Deer made a determined effort to become the capital of the new Province of Alberta, but ultimately lost out to the more influential City of Edmonton.

that many of its workers decided to build their homes close to the mill.

In October 1908 sixty-six of the people residing north of the river applied to the government to have the area incorporated as a village, largely because they felt that the local improvement district was doing too little roadwork for the amount of taxes it was collecting. Unfortunately, the petition for incorporation was flawed and was initially rejected by the government officials. Another successful attempt to form a village was made two and one-half years later.

While the settlement of North Red Deer benefited from the growth in the lumber industry as well as the work of the Catholic Church on the hill, the Town of Red Deer also received a major boost when it was designated as a divisional point by the CPR in 1907. Tens of thousands of dollars worth of improvements including a new railroad bridge, coal chutes, water tower and large addition to the roundhouse were built.

The year 1907 also saw the commission form of municipal government initiated by the town council. Under this system, two commissioners, one of whom was always the mayor, were given extensive administrative powers subject to review by the elected councillors. This new way of running the town's affairs received a hard test almost immediately when it was discovered that the secretary-treasurer had been misappropriating public funds. Ultimately, the commission system proved to be an efficient and successful form of management in a large part due to the very capable A.T. Stephenson, who was appointed as the town commissioner in July 1908.

While the community enjoyed several advances, there were a number of hardships and setbacks as well. The winter of 1906–07 was one of the harshest in recorded history, and many farmers and ranchers suffered severe losses of livestock. In the early hours of February 8, 1907, the roof of the local skating rink collapsed under a heavy weight of snow. Eighteen years would pass before another covered rink would be constructed in the community.

In the spring of 1907 the Red Deer Mill and Elevator Company—an enterprise backed by the board of trade, town council and the money of a great many local residents—dissolved into bankruptcy. In December a number of businessmen on Gaetz Avenue suffered $20,000 in losses when a spectacular fire destroyed the opera house, a furniture store, meat market and other small shops.

By early 1908 it was obvious that the boom had collapsed and a sharp recession had set in. The price for hogs and cattle dropped to less than two cents a kilogram. A number of important local businessmen went bankrupt, including one of the brickyards. In October town council refused to pay for a fountain pen purchased by the secretary-treasurer.

When the Western General proposed new rates for telephone, electrical and lighting service, town council balked and forced a hearing by an arbitration board. To the great consternation of the councillors and the community as a whole, the arbitrators granted rates higher than those originally requested by the company. A number of people angrily cancelled their phones, and public meetings were held to demand that either the provincial government or the town buy out the Western General. Town council tried to cancel its franchise agreement, but it

LEFT: In 1905 G.H. Bawtinheimer established a large sawmill in North Red Deer. In 1906 the operation was taken over by the Great West Lumber Company and became one of the largest employers in Central Alberta.

BELOW: In 1907 the CPR designated Red Deer as a main divisional point on the Calgary–Edmonton line. As part of the substantial improvements which followed, the CPR built a new steel railroad bridge across the Red Deer River.

lost its case in the courts. Ultimately, everyone was forced to accept the higher utility rates, setting the stage for the poor relations with the Western General which were to continue for several more years.

By 1909 the economy had begun to rebound, and Red Deer entered one of the strongest boom periods in its history. Much

A railway camp located just west of Red Deer and belonging to the Alberta Central Railway, a local venture. Between 1910 and 1912, two railroad companies raced each other to build rail lines to the coal fields at Nordegg.

of the growth and progress was spurred by the phenomenal amount of railroad activity in the district. The experience of 1890–1892 had shown the tremendous boost that the construction of a single rail line could bring. Now various railroad companies were announcing plans to build several more lines through the town.

The CPR had greatly increased its operations since 1907 when it had designated Red Deer as a divisional point. The construction in 1910 of a beautiful $34,000 station on the west end of Ross Street reflected the growing importance of Red Deer to the company. At the same time, the CPR proposed the construction of a branch line from Langdon to Red Deer, which would open up the districts to the south and east and make Red Deer an even greater hub of operations.

Another railroad company, the Alberta Central (ACR), was a local venture with friendly connections to the CPR. It had been chartered in 1901 to run a line from the Coalbanks (Delburne) area to the North Saskatchewan River near Rocky Mountain House. The president of the company was John T. Moore, and it is probable that his initial intention was to use the ACR to provide railroad access to the Saskatchewan Land and Homestead Company's holdings

east and west of Red Deer. The ACR's activities over the next decade, however, were largely limited to applying for time extensions to its charter and for government subsidies. As well, railroads were good politics, and John T. Moore often used the promise of the Alberta Central Railway in his election campaigns. During the 1908 federal contest he even had a surveyor plant grade stakes in politically sensitive areas.

Finally, in 1909, the federal government promised a subsidy of $4,000 per kilometre for construction of a line between Red Deer and Rocky Mountain House, and work on the ACR began in earnest. In the winter of 1909–1910, surveyors laid out a route both eastward and westward from Red Deer. In the spring, brushing and grading work began. A high point for the company and the community came in August 1910 when the Prime Minister of Canada, Sir Wilfrid Laurier, drove the first spike for the ACR at a spot on the South Hill near Gaetz Avenue.

Meanwhile, competition emerged in the form of the Canadian Northern Railroad (CNR) and its two principal promoters, William MacKenzie and Donald Mann, after whom Red Deer's MacKenzie (49th) Avenue and Mann (49th) Street had been named. These CNR magnates had joined

with the German Development Company in a venture to open up the newly discovered Brazeau coal fields west of Rocky Mountain House. They subsequently secured a provincial railroad charter under the name Canadian Northern Western Railroad (CNWR) and announced their plans to build from their line near Stettler, through the Red Deer district and west to the Brazeau.

The CNWR was in such a rush to get started that instead of commissioning extensive surveys, it copied the ones filed by the ACR with the federal Department of Railroads. The result was that the proposed routes for the two lines followed each other so closely that in one thirty mile stretch, they intersected at least five times. The federal railroad authorities ordered the CNWR to move its line farther northward. However, the two routes still closely paralleled each other, and the two companies commenced a race to see who could reach the Brazeau coal fields first.

The competition was stiff and frequently bitter. Lawsuits and countersuits were filed as the rivals tried to secure the best right-of-way. Construction crews built grades as much as two metres above those of the other company where the two lines crossed. Occasionally, violence flared up as

fist fights broke out between opposing crews. At times matters even took a comic turn. The kitchen staff of one camp decided to claim a local stray dog by clipping the letters *ACR* on its side. The dog returned the next day with the letters *CNR* clipped on the other side.

As the competition between the two companies heated up, the effect on the Town of Red Deer and the surrounding area was electrifying. The number of available jobs skyrocketed and wages soared. Local farmers found ready markets for their grain, hay and livestock at prices double and triple those offered before the boom. Merchants experienced astounding demand for their good and services and gleefully watched as their profits mushroomed. Those involved in the construction or related industries found it next to impossible to keep up with demand. The growing flood of newcomers filled all available accommodation, and people often camped out in tents until new homes could be built or purchased.

A few statistics give an indication of the extent of the boom. The Town of Red Deer's population jumped by nearly 1,000 in two years. The value of building permits issued tripled in a year and quintupled in two years. In the Village of North Red Deer the number of residents leapt from less

LEFT: On August 10, 1910, Sir Wilfrid Laurier drove the first spike for the Alberta Central Railway at a site near the current Capri Centre. Also shown in the photograph are John T. Moore, ACR President; and Minister of Railways, Hon. G.P. Graham (back to the camera).

RIGHT: Laurier's stop in Red Deer was part of a preelection political tour. A large stand was built for him to deliver his speech. However, a sudden thunderstorm soon sent the crowd scurrying for the Lyric Theatre.

ABOVE: In 1912 a local Jersey cow, Rosalind of Old Basing, set an international record for milk production. The Board of Trade held a lavish banquet in her honour.

BELOW: In 1912 the Red Deer Memorial Hospital was greatly enlarged to handle the medical needs of the rapidly growing community.

than 300 at the time of incorporation (February 1911) to more than 500 nineteen months later. The Great West Lumber Company cut less than two million board metres of lumber in 1909 and over three and a half million metres in 1912.

As the boom progressed, a number of new businesses and industries were opened. In 1909 a clothing manufacturing company, first known as Square Garments Ltd. and later as the Gaetz Manufacturing Company,

was formed. After construction of a factory on Blowers (51st) Street, it claimed to be the largest maker of overalls west of Winnipeg. In 1910 the Freytag Tannery Co. was started, and in 1911 it built a plant next to the Great West Lumber mill. In 1912 the Laurentia Milk Company was created and began the processing of milk using the new method of homogenization. This venture reflected the growing importance of the dairying industry to Central Alberta, a fact recognized by the Red Deer Board of Trade when it held a lavish banquet to honour Rosalind of Old Basing, the international record-holding Jersey cow owned by C.A. Julian Sharman.

In 1909 Dr. Richard Parsons bought the first car in Red Deer. While his McLaughlin Buick initially caused some havoc in the community by frightening teams of horses, it also initiated a flurry of automobile purchasing by several of the now prosperous townspeople. Within three years there were over four dozen cars in the community, one of the highest per capita rates of ownership in the province. This development also led to the establishment of another type of business in Red Deer: the automobile garage.

As Red Deer's commercial and industrial sectors flourished, public services were improved and expanded. New roads and streets were built and several kilometres of new waterworks were installed. In 1910 the old wooden boardwalks in the downtown area were replaced with concrete sidewalks. In 1912 the Town Hall and the Memorial Hospital were extensively renovated and enlarged.

The town also began to acquire parcels of park and recreation land, the nucleus of the now famous parks system. In 1909 H.H. Gaetz, a former mayor, donated a beautiful tract along the Red Deer River at the mouth of Waskasoo Creek. The following year town council purchased eighteen hectares on the south side of Red Deer and named it Waskasoo Park. In 1911 the ratepayers voted to take over Alexandra Park from the Exhibition Association. Extensive improvements to the fairgrounds were made the next year.

There also were important additions to Red Deer's education facilities during the boom. In 1912 the public school built two two-roomed cottage schools, one each in North and South Red Deer. At the same time, the Daughters of Wisdom built a new wing on the convent to provide additional classroom space. In January 1913 the Presbyterian Church opened a college for young women, the Alberta Ladies College, on the crest of the East Hill. Instruction was provided in standard school subjects, commercial education, domestic science, art and music, all with an emphasis on scripture study.

In 1910 the Methodists built a beautiful new church on Ross Street, which they named in honour of the late Reverend Leonard Gaetz. The old building on Blowers (51st) Street was converted into an automobile dealership and garage. In 1912 the Salvation Army came to Red Deer, and in 1913 the Pentecostal Church of the Nazarene established a congregation in the town.

Although the boom resulted in astounding progress for the community, there were some undesirable developments as well. The strong employment situation attracted a large number of transients and quite a few disreputable characters. Consequently, Red Deer's crime rate began to soar. In 1910 the local police dealt with thirty-five criminal

cases. In 1911 the number of cases leapt to nearly 200, and in 1912 the police investigated almost 250 crimes.

Most of these crimes involved the illegal sale and possession of liquor, illicit gambling and petty theft. However, a much more serious incident occurred in June 1911. A drifter named Arthur Kelly held up two businessmen late one evening. When Police Chief Bell arrived on the scene to stop the holdup, Kelly shot and seriously wounded him. A general alarm was sounded, and several armed parties of men were sent out to capture the assailant. Surprisingly it was a troop of Boy Scouts who finally discovered the

ABOVE: In 1911 and 1912, the Public School Board built frame cottage schools in North and South Red Deer as "temporary" accommodations for the burgeoning school population. This school in North Red Deer, like its mate on 45th Street, is still in use.

LEFT: In 1911 a local Boy Scout troop became famous when it helped to capture Arthur Kelly, a drifter who had shot Red Deer's police chief, George Bell.

By 1912 Red Deer had become a thriving community of nearly 3000 people. The downtown had become a hub of commercial activity for Central Alberta.

fugitive hiding in a clump of willows near the exhibition grounds. Kelly was subsequently convicted of attempted murder and was sent to jail for seven years. The Boy Scouts were each awarded with a medal by the town and two were sent to England for the King's coronation rally. Bell recovered after several weeks and received a letter from Kelly, which said in part, "Please forgive me the trick I have done to you. Hope to see you soon."

Another unfortunate development was the wild spree of real estate speculation spurred on by the boom. People felt that if Red Deer's population could increase tenfold in a decade, there was no reason why it could not continue to surge to twenty or thirty thousand in another ten years or so. Investors and speculators consequently bought up all the available land and then congratulated themselves on their wisdom as the resulting spiral of land prices created enormous paper profits.

Over a dozen new subdivisions were placed on the market by developers and real estate promoters. A number of these places were a considerable distance beyond the corporate limits of the town and would not see any true development for several decades. Many of the lots were bought by people in Eastern Canada, the United States and Great Britain for whom Red Deer was noth-

ing more than a point on the map. Even the ill-starred Saskatchewan Land and Homestead Company began to experience brisk and profitable sales.

For local residents the same boundless optimism which fuelled the real estate craze prompted many to suggest that now was the time to change Red Deer's municipal status. The prairie town of 3,000 appeared well on its way to becoming a major metropolis and only "a pessimist or a fool" would argue against Red Deer being incorporated as a city. There also was the practical consideration that debentures for a city would be easier to sell than would debentures for a town. This situation would be a tremendous boost to the financing of much-needed public works projects.

On March 10 the provincial legislature passed the required legislation. On March 25, when the Lieutenant-Governor gave his assent, Red Deer officially became a city. Curiously, the major event was not celebrated in any substantial way. The mayor had treated this council and town administrators to an oyster dinner, but no ceremony took place when incorporation actually came into force. Even the *Red Deer Advocate* devoted only a fifteen-centimetre-long column to the news.

Red Deer ironically achieved its city sta-

tus just as the boom was beginning to collapse. Warning signs had been in evidence for some time. In January 1912 the ACR had become bankrupt. While the CPR took over construction of the line, it was at a much slower pace and on a less grand scale. Work on the Langdon branch never extended farther north than the Wimbourne district. Construction of the CNWR line continued rapidly, but the rails were laid some distance north of the city. The CNR had announced plans to build another branch from Edmonton to Calgary, which would have provided connections to Red Deer. However, work on this line was limited to a small section in North Red Deer.

RED DEER, 1923

With the tremendous excitement of the great boom, the *Red Deer Advocate* published this wildly optimistic picture of what it thought Ross Street would look like in ten years.

As the spring of 1913 progressed, the economy began to decline noticeably. The pace of new construction slowed, workers were laid off and a spiral of unemployment began. Businesses started to go bankrupt. Artificially high land prices collapsed, and speculators as well as many ordinary citizens found themselves unable to pay their taxes on the land which they had so eagerly purchased only a short time before.

During the 1913 provincial election, Red Deer's MLA and leader of the provincial Conservative Party, Edward Michener, found himself in a close contest with his Liberal opponent, R.B. Welliver. Michener consequently convinced his friends and allies in the federal government to announce the construction of an armoury and a lavish new post office building for Red Deer. After a brief but fierce public controversy over location, the armoury was constructed on the southeast corner of the City Square. Work on the new post office, however, never progressed past the excavation of a large hole next to the land titles office. Meanwhile, Michener managed to get reelected but with a plurality of just over 100 votes.

The boost from the federal public works projects proved to be short-lived. By the end of the year Red Deer was in the depths of a serious recession. The banks were refusing to supply the city with any more credit and debentures would not sell. In the words of Mayor F.W. Galbraith, the "millionaires" of the previous year were starting to worry about how they would be able to buy fuel for the coming winter.

As the grim winter of 1913–1914 turned into spring, there was a dramatic turn of events. On May 14, 1914, the A.W. Dingman well at Turner Valley blew in. The largest oil and gas field in the British Empire had been discovered. A surge of oil fever followed the news of the strike.

Although Red Deer was over 200 kilometres north of the find, a wave of excitement swept the community. People made the logical supposition that if there was all that oil and gas at Turner Valley, there was probably plenty in Central Alberta as well. Now there was a chance of sudden wealth and economic salvation.

People rushed into the local land office to make sure they did not miss out on the expected bonanza. In a community which had appeared cash-starved only a fortnight before, $45,000 in leases were snapped up in a week and one-half. The beleaguered real estate agents became stockbrokers and promoters overnight. City council, seeing a golden opportunity, set a new license fee of $25 for local brokers and $50 for nonresidents. There were predictable screams of outrage from the real estate community, but money quickly poured into the city's coffers.

As the boom progressed, local oil companies were formed, and their shares were placed on the market. The first of these was the Red Deer Oil and Gas Co. with Central Alberta Oils and Innisfail Pioneer Oil Co. being organized shortly thereafter. Meanwhile, prices for shares in southern Alberta oil companies continued to skyrocket.

On June 18, 1914, the oil frenzy reached its peak with the news that the Monarch well, 120 kilometres southwest of Red Deer, had struck oil. People stampeded to the

land titles office to register for the priority number now needed to file for a lease. The editor of the *Advocate* bet an alderman a box of cigars that the lineup would not exceed 500. He lost. By the end of the day, over 600 had applied for a number. The following morning 400 more registered.

It was the climax of the boom. Within a month share prices began to plummet and the demand for leases evaporated. By the end of July the Red Deer Oil and Gas Company had suspended operations. Two other companies started drilling south of Red Deer, but both of these wells were failures.

For a brief time it had appeared that the old boom had made a glorious return. Now, in retrospect, the oil boom looked like a brief but spectacular encore before the curtain finally closed on a golden era. While people were caught up with oil fever, the CNWR finished its line to Nordegg, and the CPR completed the ACR line as far as Rocky Mountain House. The railroad construction bonanza was now over. While the land titles office was swamped with demands for oil leases, few people noticed that the number of homestead entries had plunged. The settlement era was drawing to a close.

As the economy began to swing downward once again, events thousands of kilometres away began to spiral out of control.

On June 28, 1914, the Austrian Archduke Francis Ferdinand was assassinated at Sarajevo. On August 4 Great Britain and its empire declared war on Germany. The attention of Red Deer now turned to this terrible conflict, one of the worst in the history of mankind.

At the height of the oil fever of 1914, hundreds of people lined up at Red Deer's land titles office, hoping to register their speculative leases.

During the great oil frenzy of 1914, several companies such as Central Alberta Oils Limited were formed. Within a year, virtually every one of them had folded.

Chapter 5

The Great War

LEFT: During the First World War several military units trained at the Fairgrounds. Pictured here on the racetrack is C Squadron of the 12th Canadian Mounted Rifles in 1915.

ABOVE: Program for the farewell ball for the 89th Battalion CEF.

War. It was a cataclysm which had not touched Central Alberta since the end of the Boer War, a dozen years before. Ironically, Red Deer had joined in a celebration of peace in October 1913. Now, in the words of the *Red Deer News*, the community faced "the most terrible war since the fall of the Roman Empire."

Word of the declaration of war reached Red Deer around 8 P.M. on August 4, 1914. The following evening the community responded to the news with a large spontaneous public demonstration. The Red Deer Band, which had been out for its weekly practice, led a kilometre-long procession to the armoury on the City Square. For the next three hours there were loud impromptu speeches, passionate choruses of songs and general eruptions of patriotic excitement.

The local squadron of militia, the 35th Central Alberta Horse, greeted the news of the war with equal enthusiasm. Although the squadron had been in existence for only a year and one-half, it immediately wired to the Minister Militia its willingness and readiness to serve. It also commenced nightly

**"C" Squadron
12th C. M. R.**

"It's an awful folly
"Not to be jolly
"That's what we think"

Ladies Receiving

MESDAMES H.L.GAETZ, H.E.WHITE,
F. HOLT, R. GEE

Red Deer, May 7th, 1915

As the regiments and battalions left Red Deer, farewell balls and receptions were held for the soldiers. The slogans were often naively cheerful and optimistic.

drills and practices at the armoury. On August 21, the day after the soldiers were honoured at the Red Deer Fair, orders were received for seventy-five men to depart for the war. A large, sometimes tearful crowd saw the young men off on the train.

After the departure of the first contingent, the militia continued with the recruitment and training of volunteers. In October Red Deer was designated as a main recruiting station for Central Alberta, and by November over 200 men had applied for enlistment. There was some consternation when the military authorities indicated that as few as fifty volunteers might be called up for the second contingent. Several young men worried that the war would be over before they had a chance to get overseas.

On November 19, 1914, sixty-four recruits from Red Deer and district left for Calgary to train with the 31st Battalion. Once again, an enormous crowd gathered to bid them farewell. After the soldiers' departure it was reported that they had been given comfortable billets in the swine building at the Calgary Exhibition grounds. An office wrote that it was the best accommodation in the camp.

While the military was busy with mobilization, the community busied itself with the organization of the home front. In early September a local patriotic fund was established to support the dependants of soldiers on active service. Within a month over $5,000 was subscribed for the fund. Food, clothing and other essentials were also collected for the Belgian Relief Fund. The community responded generously. Arrangements were made to send a carload of wheat. One local real estate company even donated forty-five cases of canned milk from the Laurentia Milk Company, which had recently closed, partly because of spoilage in its product.

City council reacted to the outbreak of war by redoubling its program of financial restraint. City staff were asked to accept pay cuts of between 20 and 40 percent. Some employees such as the public works foreman, the sanitary inspector and the parks superintendent were laid off. One new project, however, was allowed to proceed. In November 1914 the Red Deer Public Library opened in the old Board of Trade offices in the City Hall building.

As the fall progressed, the local newspapers were full of news of the terrible battles being waged in Belgium and France. The Gaetz Cornett Drug and Bookstore had a special telegraph wire installed and posted the latest war bulletin in its windows. The Lyric Theatre became the first establishment in Alberta to show movies of the war. Some local residents received the tragic news of the deaths of overseas relatives, and in December the community learned that one member of the first contingent, Francis Ross, had died of spinal meningitis in Scotland. The reality of the war was beginning to take hold.

As 1914 drew to a close, the military authorities indicated that another squadron of mounted infantry would be raised and trained at Red Deer. City council quickly offered the use of the Exhibition Park as training quarters, but the onset of cold weather prevented the immediate acceptance of the proposal. In January 1915, when recruitment for C Squadron of the 12th Canadian Mounted Rifles (CMR) commenced, temporary billets were provided in the armoury, and arrangements for meals were made at the Commercial and Olympia cafes. Once spring arrived, however, the men were moved to their new quarters at the fairgrounds. The livestock buildings were converted into barracks, and the horticul-

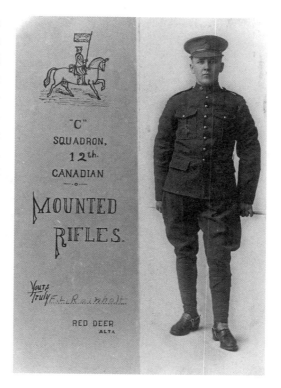

"C" SQUADRON, 12th. CANADIAN

MOUNTED RIFLES.

Yours Truly E.L.Rainholt

RED DEER ALTA

LEFT: Prior to leaving for overseas many soldiers had their photos taken as mementoes for their families and friends.

tural building was used as a dining hall. The medical health officer also arranged to have the men inoculated for typhoid fever.

While the members of the 12th CMR were settling into their new quarters, the Canadians of the First Division were embroiled in the terrible Battle of Ypres, the first battle in which poisonous gas was used as a weapon. By May the Red Deer newspapers were full of accounts of local men

BELOW: With the cramped training facilities at the start of the war, some troops were forced to conduct their exercises on Ross and other nearby streets.

In 1915 the highest flood ever recorded on the Red Deer River swamped the Western General power plant next to the CPR bridge.

being killed or wounded in action. The tragedy of the war was now striking home.

On May 17, 1915, word was received that the second contingent had arrived safely in England. Five days later the soldiers of the 12th CMR departed from Red Deer. A crowd estimated at between 1,500 and 2,000 gathered at the station to see the young men off. The Red Deer Citizens Band played a number of farewell tunes, but there were no formal speeches or rounds of cheering.

During the last week of June torrential rains caused the Red Deer River to rise by nearly six metres, the highest level in recorded history. A large section of Riverside Drive (Waskasoo Crescent) was washed away, and the Western General's power plant was flooded out. In North Red Deer the Great West Lumber Company's dam and mill pond were damaged, and the Canadian Northern's railbed was badly eroded.

The damage the CNR suffered was but one more setback to its plans to extend its rail line into Red Deer. Financial conditions for the company were poor. Earlier in 1915 city council had been approached for some major concessions, including the cancellation of a $3,000 debt, the granting of a site for a stockyard and the payment of $42,000 to the Townsite Company for a right-of-way. The city faced severe financial prob-

lems of its own and sharply turned down the CNR's request.

Coincidentally, the very wet weather struck Red Deer three weeks before a provincial plebiscite on the prohibition of alcohol. Despite their sodden surroundings, the citizens of Red Deer voted "dry" by a margin of over 80 percent, while the rest of the province approved of prohibition by a margin of only 61 percent. In the words of the editor of the *Advocate*, himself a strong prohibitionist, the results showed "how strongly public sentiment has become ranged against the barroom parasite."

While the heavy rains initially caused some havoc and disruption, they also gave a tremendous boost to the local crops. The late summer and fall turned warm and dry, and consequently the district's farmers were able to harvest the largest bumper crop in the history of Central Alberta. The tremendous increase in production across Western Canada caused some decline in agricultural prices. However, the crop yields were so astounding that farmers still experienced one of their best years since settlement began.

The new prosperity for farmers meant an improved economy for Red Deer. Another boost came when two wholesale grocery companies announced plans to build large warehouses in the city. These were the first

major construction projects to be undertaken since the boom had collapsed in 1913. They also reflected the growing role of Red Deer as the major distribution point for Central Alberta.

While economic conditions improved somewhat, the situation with municipal finances remained poor. Tax arrears for 1915 amounted to $49,000 on top of another $73,000 in uncollected taxes from the previous two years. Debenture debt totalled over $370,000, and there was an unpaid bill of $2,800 to the Western General for electrical power and street lighting.

Incredibly, given the state of the city's finances, city council became involved in negotiations to purchase the Western General's power plant and assets. There was considerable resentment over the company's rates of twenty cents per kilowatt hour, which were one-third higher than those in other communities. The franchise agreement of 1903 now gave the city an opportunity to buy out the utility.

The city's bankers were appalled. The per capita debt was already $124, and the purchase of the Western General would raise it to $207. The Bank of Montreal wrote that the proposal "should not be considered for one moment" and that any agreement to purchase "would seriously impair the credit of the city."

At a special public meeting held in September, the assembled ratepayers voted in favour of buying out the Western General by a margin of two votes. The mayor, John Carswell, who was adamantly opposed to the proposal, called for a second vote which resulted in a tie and a great deal of controversy. City council ultimately agreed to offer the Western General $200,000 by a vote of three to two with one of the consenting aldermen being an employee of the company. The Western General held that its assets and franchise were worth at least $250,000 and flatly refused the city's offer. The old franchise agreement and an atmosphere of acrimony continued for another decade.

The Western General Electric power plant on the west side of Gaetz Avenue. The proposal to purchase the company by the City of Red Deer became one of the community's most heated controversies.

A common sight during the First World War was soldiers marching from the armoury along Mann (49th) Street toward the train station where they departed for overseas.

During the summer of 1915 a number of Red Deer and district men enlisted in the 63rd and 66th Battalions, which were mainly raised in the Edmonton area. In the fall the military authorities announced the recruitment of the 89th Battalion, two companies of which were to be stationed and trained at Red Deer.

Once again arrangements were made to use the exhibition grounds as training quarters. However, there were now 500 men to be accommodated instead of 150 as had been the case with the 12th CMR. The city found it necessary to undertake $2,000 in renovations and improvements. These included the installation of a water main to the site and the construction of both a new 280 square metre building and a large addition to the exhibits hall. The city managed to save $200 by constructing unlined buildings instead of insulated ones. The city commissioner noted that in the future the structures would "come in useful for increased stock requirements at the Fair."

The new water main to the fairgrounds was installed after the onset of cold weather, and the camp was plagued throughout the winter by frozen and burst pipes. The winter of 1915–1916 was a very cold one, and problems with frozen waterworks were common in other parts of the city as well. People responded by running their taps continuously in order to keep their lines from freezing. Unfortunately, as a result, it often became impossible to keep adequate water pressure for fire protection. The Western General also complained about the large increase in water consumption and asked the city to consider the installation of water meters.

In February 1916 the city officially unveiled an honour roll with the names of over 430 young men who had enlisted for the war, eighteen of whom had already lost their lives. Shortly thereafter the Methodist Church and the Masonic Lodge unveiled rolls of honour for their members. These lists were far from being closed. The car-

nage of Flanders and other battlefields had increased the demand for fresh recruits. Earlier recruitments had been for a few dozen men, a squadron and then a company. Now the military authorities announced plans to mobilize a whole battalion, the 187th, in Central Alberta.

Recruitment for the 187th commenced on April 26, 1916. Although the *Red Deer Advocate* had written that Alberta's cities and towns were cleaned out of young men and the farm labour shortage was such that members of the 89th Battalion had been sent out to help with the spring farm work, the response was amazing. Within ten days over 250 volunteers had enlisted. By June 16, when a special ceremony was held in Innisfail to present the colours of the 187th Battalion, over 550 recruits had signed up.

Temporary billets were provided in the armoury for the Red Deer volunteers, but these accommodations were soon filled to capacity. After the departure of the two companies of the 89th Battalion on May 25, the men of the 187th were moved to the quarters at the fairgrounds where the city had started to build yet another large barn.

Facilities were still stretched to the limit during the first week of July when the annual fair was held. The crowds were the largest in years. There were more exhibits than ever

before and special tents had to be pitched to handle all the livestock entries. Not surprisingly, the major attraction of the fair was the 187th Battalion. The soldiers put on demonstrations of military manoeuvres and acrobatics. As well, during the grand parade the recruits were joined by two young women who carried a banner that said, "If you can join the 187th Battalion but won't, wear this"—"this" being a woman's skirt and a white feather.

The 187th was dubbed the Veterans' Battalion because ten of the officers were veterans of the Boer War and several had already seen service in the current war. Unfortu-

ABOVE: The 89th Battalion CEF, like other units trained in Red Deer during the war, found that the infield at the fairgrounds made an excellent parade square.

BELOW: Cooks from the 12th CMR often faced uncertain water supply and poor sanitary conditions.

Edward Michener, Red Deer's second MLA, had the honour of presenting the regimental colours to the 187th Battalion in 1916. The colours are currently kept in St. Mark's Anglican Church in Innisfail.

nately, one of the sergeants developed a fatal case of typhoid fever shortly after the Battalion left Red Deer for Calgary in mid-July. The medical health officers had the city's drinking water analyzed to see if it was responsible, but the test came back negative. A detective was later hired and reported to city council that since the strain of typhoid was not one usually found in Western Canada, it was probable that the germs had been placed by an enemy agent in the food consumed by the officers.

While accommodations were tight for the military in Red Deer, they were practically nonexistent for the civilian population. Prohibition removed one of the main sources of income for the local hotels. As a result, by June 1916 both the Alexandra and Windsor hotels had closed their doors and the Arlington was in a turmoil as the managers tried to break their lease with the owners. Only the Alberta Hotel was fully operational, but many of its rooms were taken up by lodgers. The problem was com-

pounded by the fact that it was not possible to take a train to Red Deer and leave on another on the same day.

One special group which experienced accommodation problems was comprised of men who had returned home from active service, usually because of wounds received at the front. In December 1915 a special committee was established by city council, the board of trade and the Patriotic Fund to care for these returned veterans. Within a few weeks public appeals were being made by the committee for temporary homes for convalescent soldiers.

Meanwhile, the situation with the city's finances had become critical. Of $95,000 in taxes owed in 1916, the city was able to collect only $34,000. With the exception of properties owned by soldiers on active service, any land which had two years of arrears against it could be sold in a tax sale. However, a number of people paid the minimum amount of arrears necessary to have the property removed from the sale, and any

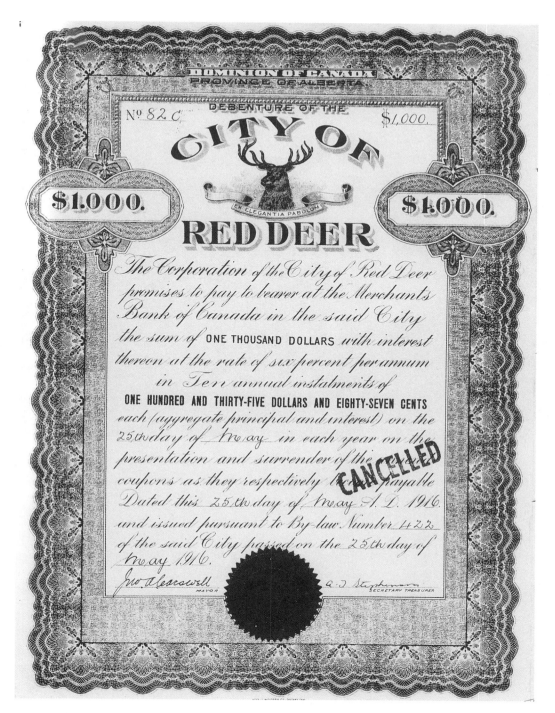

land which the city did seize simply would not sell on the open market.

By June 1916 the city still owed the public school board nearly $9,000 from the 1915 tax requisition and the separate school and hospital boards another $1,200. The Western General was owed over $5,000 for power and lighting, and the Forest City Paving Company had not received payment on a disputed bill of over $4,000. The over-draft at the bank reached $58,000, and the Bank of Montreal consequently refused to grant any further credit. In short, the city was broke.

Because Red Deer's problems were not unique, the provincial government stepped in and gave the city the power to issue trea-sury bills secured by the amount of tax arrears. City council decided to sell $55,000 of these treasury bills to cover its debts.

The switchboard of the Western General Telephone office in 1916. This locally owned company found it increasingly difficult to keep up with technological changes in the telephone business. Pressure to sell out to Alberta Government Telephones consequently increased.

Unfortunately, this decision was based on the premise that the money raised would tide over the nonpayment of taxes until property values returned to "normal." What was considered to be normal was the overinflated values of the land frenzy of 1911–1913.

The city administration was not the only part of the community facing financial hardships. Local contributions to the Patriotic Fund had been among the highest in the province, but the fund was still paying out hundreds of dollars more than it was taking in. Moreover, nearly $600 in pledges were in arrears. The Alberta Ladies College had $63,500 in unpaid subscriptions and the board of trustees finally found it impossible to keep the college operating in Red Deer. The building was sold to the provincial government for $125,000 in the spring of 1916, and classes were moved to temporary quarters at the University of Alberta in Edmonton.

The provincial government initially planned to use the college building as a home for mentally handicapped children.

However, many of the men returning from the war were suffering from terrible injuries to their minds as well as from wounds to their bodies. Consequently, the government decided, at least temporarily, to turn the facility into a mental hospital for convalescent soldiers.

During the summer of 1916 the Canadian Northern Railroad began to work again on the extension of the Brazeau line into Red Deer. The grade damaged by the heavy rains of 1915 was repaired and construction of a bridge across the Red Deer River was started. Unfortunately, the ill-starred project continued to be beset by problems. Bridge work was delayed by a shortage of steel, and the contractors were plagued by a chronic shortage of labour. The fall of 1916 was nearly as wet as the spring of 1915. Consequently, the hillsides began to slip, the grade was badly eroded and a three-metre-high flood on the river damaged the bridge piers. Moreover, the financial condition of the company continued to deteriorate to

the extent that the CNR was totally bank-rupt within a few months.

As the fall of 1916 progressed Red Deer's newspapers were full of reports of the heavy casualties at the terrible Battle of the Somme. There was a last minute recruitment drive in late September to bring the 187th Battalion up to full strength. However, it was becoming obvious in both Central Alberta and Canada as a whole that voluntary recruitment could no longer meet the needs of the armies now locked in a bloody struggle of attrition.

At the end of October the 191st Battalion arrived in Red Deer for winter training although there was some reluctance on the part of the military authorities to use the exhibition grounds again. The city, despite its poor financial position, agreed to make further improvements, including the construction of new accommodations for the senior officers and the fitting-up of sergeants' quarters. A thick coating of manure was placed over the water main to prevent any further

freezing problems. Bacteriological analyses of the city's water were sent to military district headquarters in Calgary.

Nevertheless, rumours persisted that the Battalion was to be relocated to Calgary. City council finally sent a telegram to the Prime Minister of Canada, who replied that there had never been any intention of moving the Battalion. Unfortunately, at the end of December, problems developed with the cesspool between the sergeants' mess and one of the barracks. A whole company of men had to be temporarily evacuated to the Alexandra Hotel. Although the problems were cleared up by the second week of January, orders were suddenly given on January 18 that the 191st was to leave for Calgary before the end of the weekend. The military authorities ended their leasing arrangement, and after cleaning up the site and buildings, turned the fairgrounds back to the city at the beginning of May 1917.

The 191st was the last major unit to be stationed in Red Deer during the war. Some

The CPR station and yards were often the scene of heartwrenching farewells as the young men of the community departed for the trenches of the Western Front.

Soldiers in the aftermath of the Battle of Vimy Ridge in April 1917. They participated in the greatest Canadian victory of the Great War. While the battle became a symbol of Canadian skill and spirit, it also involved a heavy loss of life.

recruitment continued for such battalions as the 223rd (Scandinavian) and for such services as the Royal Canadian Navy and the Royal Flying Corps. However, voluntary recruitment began to seriously flag. Early in 1917 the National Service Board tried to make a nation-wide inventory of manpower. It passed on the information it received to local recruiting officers, but the results were very disappointing. In Red Deer a local farmer was fined $100 for frightening away potential recruits by telling stories of the horrors of the front.

In April 1917 the Canadian Corps, fighting for the first time with all four division, captured the strategic Vimy Ridge in northern France. The battle was Canada's greatest victory of the war and became a symbol of Canadian skill and spirit. It was also an achievement with a tragic cost. Twelve men from Red Deer and district were killed on the first day of the attack, Easter Monday. Sixteen others lost their lives during the rest of the battle. The Canadian Corps as a whole suffered nearly 11,000 casualties at Vimy, of which 3,600 were killed. On May 18, 1917, Prime Minister Borden announced that compulsory military service would be introduced.

Conscription was an explosive political issue which shattered traditional partisan loyalties. Red Deer had been fairly evenly split between the Conservatives and the Liberals. In the spring of 1917, Edward Michener, Red Deer's MLA and provincial leader of the Conservative Party, was reelected by a plurality of only thirty-one votes. A few weeks later, however, Dr. Michael Clark, Red Deer's Liberal member of parliament, announced his support of conscription and joined the new Union Government of Conservative Prime Minister Borden.

While the debate over conscription heated up, the Canadian troops were embroiled in the muddy, bloody and futile Battle of Passchendaele in Flanders. Sixteen thousand men were killed or wounded, including twenty from Red Deer and district. The war had taken on a new gruesome intensity, which made the shortage of manpower even more acute.

In December 1917 Canadians endorsed conscription by reelecting the Union government. In Red Deer Dr. Clark was returned with a resounding majority of over 1,200 votes. Despite this indication of public support, conscription failed to produce the hoped-for results. Over 400,000 men were registered under the Military Service Act, but only one-quarter of these entered the military. Only 24,000 men were ultimately sent to the front.

There was also an element of capriciousness with which the applications for exemptions were handled. One Red Deer applicant was judged to be fit for service despite medical certification of heart problems. An Alberta Government Telephones lineman was denied exemption despite a claim by his employer that long-distance telephone service would greatly suffer if he left his work. A theological student was excused by the local tribunal when it was decided that only German Lutherans would be left to pastor his congregation if he were called up. During the federal election campaign, the government promised that all farmers actively involved in food production would not be conscripted. Five months later these exemptions were cancelled.

While conscription of men was being debated and implemented, there were strong public demands for the conscription of wealth as well. The federal government had attempted to meet most of its financial demands by heavy borrowings. The Third Canada War Loan and Victory Loan campaigns of 1917 were successful in raising over one-half billion dollars. In April 1917, however, the Minister of Finance yielded to the growing strains of the war effort and implemented two "temporary" measures: a business profits tax and a personal income tax.

PATRIOTIC AUCTION SALE AND SUPPER

=== At the Armouries ===

Under the auspices of the Local Council of Women,

SATURDAY, OCTOBER 21, 1916

AFTERNOON AND EVENING

Many useful articles will be offered for sale, such as :

Baled hay, load coal, split wood, fence posts, green feed, turkeys, ducks, chickens, purebred Rhode Island Red roosters, butter, eggs, cheese, fresh fruits, canned fruit, vegetables, table meats, groceries, apples, whiffeltrees, Royal Crown soap, shovels, fire extinguishers, furniture, fancy work, china, stationery, fancy articles, dolls clothes, new dry goods, complete set of false teeth to order, wall-paper, Laurentia homogenized milk, house plants, silver berry spoon, cutlery, brass hot water kettle with alcohol lamp, Indian bead work, mounted Loon, electric iron, Moir's chocalates and other candy, peanuts, electric toaster, electric bulbs,

and many other useful and staple articles too numerous to mention.

Afternoon Tea	
Sandwiches	5c
Cake	5c
Doughnuts	5c
Tea	5c
Coffee....	5c
Pie	5c
Served Afternoon & Evening	

Hot Supper	
Scalloped Potatoes....	5c
Creamed "	5c
Baked Beans	5c
Cold Ham & Chicken	10c
Tea or Coffee	5c
Pie	5c
Served from 5:30 p.m. on	

Attractions and Amusements

Ding Dong Bell   The Chocolate Ladies   Punch and Judy Show   Baby Show
Fortune Telling   Ball Games   B.C. Apple Pie Contest   Etc.

COME FOR SUPPER AND SPEND THE EVENING

The proceeds will be used to send Xmas Field Comforts direct to all our soldiers overseas from Red Deer and District

FREE—ADMISSION—FREE

GOD SAVE THE KING !

While the federal government was striving to manage its financial problems, the City of Red Deer's fiscal position reached another crisis point. Uncollected taxes for 1917 reached $48,000, and the city defaulted on some of its debenture payments. A special franchise tax levied against the Western General was disallowed by the courts except for the portion payable to the public school district. The city's bankers finally cut off all

Many groups such as the Patriotic Fund and the Red Deer Local Council of Women held charity events to raise funds for the soldiers overseas.

credit, and teachers' salaries were paid by the public school board only after some private individuals took out notes in their own names. Fortunately, the city managed to find a new bank which was willing to handle its accounts, albeit with a strict overdraft limit. As well, $30,000 in new treasury bills were sold to meet expenses.

Ironically, while the city's financial position was desperate, it was forced to provide its employees with special $10 per month allowances because of a growing spiral of inflation. The wartime shortages of material, produce and labour contributed to the escalating cost of living, and the massive borrowings being made by all levels of government added to the inflationary pressures. By late 1917 many local businessmen were forced to suspend credit accounts as they adjusted to the new economic realities.

Nevertheless, there were many bright spots in Central Alberta's economy. Farmers enjoyed outstanding prices for their grain and livestock, and their prosperity improved the profits and incomes of the townspeople of Red Deer. Sales of farmland became brisk, and land prices began to move upward for the first time since 1913. With so many young men away fighting in the war, there was not a corresponding increase in prospective homesteaders, and in March 1918 the Dominion Land Titles office was closed.

The lingering slump in construction activity and the acute shortage of labour caused the Great West Lumber Company finally to fold in early 1917. The improved economic prospects, however, led the Manning–Sutherland Lumber Company to open a yard on the south side of Red Deer in January 1918. This development added to Red Deer's status as a regional retail and distribution centre.

Automobile sales increased dramatically in late 1916 and in 1917 despite the fact that Ford touring cars sold for $495 and a Chevrolet Four Ninety cost nearly $700.

Unfortunately, all these new cars on the road created new problems. The *Red Deer Advocate* in November 1917 complained that reckless auto driving was "keeping some citizens in terror of their lives."

Driving infractions constituted virtually the only increase in lawlessness in the community. Only two people were incarcerated in the city's cells in all of 1917. The city's police force's typical investigations involved only bylaw infractions and health code violations. The few criminal cases which did occur were handled by the newly formed Alberta Provincial Police, which took over quarters in the old Wigwam Men's Club on Gaetz Avenue and McLeod (54th) Street. All the court cases were heard in the old Gaetz Manufacturing Company building, which had been converted into a courthouse by the provincial government in early 1916.

While criminal activity in Red Deer had dropped to insignificant levels, there was a tremendous uproar when the city received three applications to open poolrooms. The local Social Service League viewed these establishments as "menaces to the community" and one member offered the opinion that "pool rooms were worse than bar rooms." A resolution was passed asking that a social centre be established "in which the young men of Red Deer might find profitable recreation under proper supervision. . . ." There was considerable debate over who might be responsible for organizing such a centre, but nothing concrete was done.

Family entertainment in Red Deer did receive a tremendous boost in July 1917 when the first Chautauqua came to the city. This travelling show offered dramatic productions, musical entertainments and educational lectures. Unfortunately, the 1917 Chautauqua was held during the same week as the annual Red Deer Fair. The program times of the two attractions were juggled to minimize conflicts, and the crowds were sufficiently large that it was agreed to make the Chautauqua an annual event in Red Deer.

The summer of 1917 also saw the formation of a veterans' organization in Red Deer. A meeting had been held in March 1917 to create the European War Veterans Association of Red Deer and District. However, following the founding convention of the Great War Veterans Association (GWVA) in Winnipeg in April, it was decided to organize a chapter of the latter organization instead. The inaugural meeting of the GWVA was held on August 17, 1917. Although there were just ten veterans present, the tiny room where the meeting was held contained only two chairs and most of the men were forced to sit on the floor. Despite these humble beginnings, club rooms were rented in the old D.S. Long harness shop on Ross Street, and a pool table was installed for the use of the members. Arrangements were also made to rent the armoury for such events as fund-raising dances.

While the GWVA was formed as an advocacy and benevolent organization for returned soldiers, there were a number of other groups and organizations which continued to provide assistance and services to the men overseas. These included the Red Cross, the International Order of the Daughters of the Empire (IODE), the Alexandra Club, the Young Men's Christian Association (YMCA), the Salvation Army, the Soldiers' Wives Club, the Red Deer Women's Institute, the Eastern Star, the Local Council of Women, the Women's Christian Temperance Union (WCTU) and a half-dozen church societies. Parcels of food, clothing and personal amenities were sent overseas as were innumerable cards and letters. Both individually and as a whole, the work of these groups provided an outstanding example of charitable community cooperation and effort.

In March 1918 the German armies, bolstered with troops transferred from the old Russian front, launched a major and initial-ly successful offensive across the Western Front. The Allied forces were forced to retreat from such hard-won positions as Passchendaele. The outlook of the war had turned very bleak.

The shortage of men for the military became even more critical. In April all single men between the ages of twenty and twenty-three were called up. In May all nineteen-year-old men were ordered to register under the Military Service Act. Shortages of food were also becoming a major problem, and attempts were made to restrict

RED DEER CHAUTAUQUA

JUNE 25 to 30

LECTURES
Brilliant
Instructive
Informative

ENTERTAINMENT
Wholesome
Artistic
Humorous

MRS. MARIE VARNEY
London, England, is still the financial centre of the world, and from that centre comes Mrs. Varney with a wealth of knowledge for the people of Western Canada. She has travelled extensively throughout Europe and has lived for some time in Paris. Mrs. Varney has won great distinction in England as a lecturer—or rather, as a woman with a definite message for mankind. In her lecture for Canadian audiences—"The Great World Heart"—she will speak of conditions in Europe and how they effect us on this continent. The British Council writes concerning her: "Besides being a speaker of great ability and distinction, the charm of Mrs. Varney's personality is most contagious, and very heartily the British Council commend her to the British public, feeling that she has a mission for the people of the British Empire."

CLAUDE SCHELL
"A Gifted Tenor Appearing with the Going-Bell-Epperson Company."
Mr. Claude Schell is a brilliant tenor and a pupil of the distinguished Herbert Witherspoon, former Metropolitan Opera Star. Lovers of good music will not be disappointed in Mr. Schell; he has sunced many notable successes on account of that resonance and exceptional smoothness of tone which distinguishes his singing In company with the Misses Going, Bell and Epperson, a brilliant programme will be given of great variety, of artistic merit and of pleasing entertainment features.

LOOK AT THIS PROGRAMME

SEASON TICKET PRICES
Adults, $3.00 · · Child's, $1.00
Tax Extra Where Levied by Province

FIRST DAY
Afternoon—
Children's Parade from four to six.
Evening—
Announcements—Chautauqua Superintendent.
Artistic and Dramatic—Calgary Kiddies' Presentation.
Admission, 25c.

SECOND DAY
Afternoon—
Concert—Florenz Company.
Admission, 50c.
Evening—
Prelude—Florenz Company.
Lecture—"Getting by your Hoodoo," Sam Grathwell
A straight message from an optimist.
Admission, 75c.

THIRD DAY
Afternoon—
Entertainment—Swiss Alpine Yodlers.
Admission, 75c.
Evening—
Prelude—Swiss Alpine Yodlers.
Lecture—"The Great World Heart," Mrs. Marie Varney.
A survey of conditions in England and Europe by a personal observer.
Admission, 75c.

FOURTH DAY
Afternoon—
Concert—Going-Epperson-Bell Company and Claude Schell, noted tenor.
Admission, 50c.
Evening—
Prelude—Going-Epperson-Bell Company and Claude Schell, Tenor.
Lecture—"Allenby in Palestine and Lawrence in Arabia." Frederic Poole.
Admission, 75c.

FIFTH DAY
Afternoon—
Grand Concert—Cheney Concert Company.
Admission, 75c.
Evening—
Prelude—Cheney Concert Company.
Lecture—"The Mission of the Anglo-Saxon Race," Daniel F. Fox. An account of the supremacy of Anglo-Saxon democracy and the contribution they can render to the world in the future.
Admission, 75c.

SIXTH DAY
Afternoon—
Prelude—Hadley Concert Company.
Lecture—"The Energies of the Universe," A. D. Carpenter. A simple and scientific account of the mysteries of the Universe.
Admission, 75c.
Evening—
Operatic Concert—Hadley Concert Company.
Admission, 75c.

ALL FOR $3.00
Get Your Tickets Now.

In 1917 the first Chautauqua was staged in Red Deer, bringing with it a new form of dramatic and musical entertainment as well as educational lectures.

by the federal government, created a tremendous backlash among voters. In a provincial by-election held after Edward Michener was appointed to the Senate in the spring of 1918, the local Unionist candidate was so badly defeated by his Liberal opponent that he lost his deposit.

While the problems of the war intensified, the city remained mired in its financial morass. The upturn in the local economy did not result in an appreciable increase in tax collections. Although the federal government asked municipalities to reduce their borrowings to allow more room for war bonds, the city was forced in May 1918 to issue another $24,000 in treasury bills to meet expenses. Moreover, the escalating rate of inflation compelled the city raise the salaries of its employees to levels approaching those paid in 1914.

As severe as the city's problems had become, they paled in comparison to the ones which plagued the Memorial Hospital. In fourteen years of operation the hospital had managed to show a surplus only twice, and both times the amounts had been a few hundred dollars. Board meetings were held only sporadically, and the auditor pointed out that there was just one paid-up member of the hospital corporation. Matters deteriorated so badly that the board chairman stated that with the exceptions of the work of the nursing superintendent and the support of local women's volunteer organizations, the management of the hospital had become "a joke."

Changes to Red Deer's city charter in 1916 and new provincial hospital legislation in 1918 allowed the city to assume more authority over the hospital. The old Memorial Hospital board was subsequently dissolved and city council appointed a three-person commission in its place. One of the first acts of the new board was to raise the patient fees in order to reduce the deficit and to meet the salary increases necessitated by a growing shortage of nurses.

E. MICHENER, M.P.P. FOR RED DEER

By 1918 Edward Michener, Red Deer's MLA and leader of the opposition in the provincial legislature, had grown tired of the closely fought electoral battles in his home constituency. He subsequently accepted an appointment to the Canadian Senate.

consumption of meat and grain products. At the same time there was a concerted effort to step up food production across the country. In Red Deer the Horticultural Society renewed the program it had started in 1917 of planting gardens in the numerous vacant lots around the city.

Ironically, while government was attempting to boost agricultural output, it cancelled the exemptions from military service for farmers. This move, combined with other unpopular measures and policies adopted

By the summer of 1918 the great German offensive had ground to a halt and new offensives by the Allied forces began to achieve results previously thought to be unattainable. German resistance weakened, then crumbled. The tide of the war had turned dramatically toward the long hoped-for final victory.

On July 31, 1918, the Red Deer Agricultural Society held one of the most successful fairs in its history. Thousands of people flocked to the fairgrounds to watch Katherine Stinson make the first airplane landing in Red Deer's history. One week later the Chautauqua came to Red Deer. Once again, large crowds turned out to take in the attractions and entertainment.

By fall the local newspapers were full of reports of the continuing successes of the Canadian and Allied troops. There was also the disturbing news of a rapidly spreading epidemic of Spanish influenza. This new and terrible disease initially caused symptoms deceptively similar to the common cold. Within a brief period of time, however, a high fever and intense soreness of muscles set in. Delirium frequently developed and many victims of the flu soon succumbed to pneumonia or other fatal complications. Tragically, people in their twenties and thirties, the age group which had suffered most of the casualties of the war, seemed to be the most vulnerable to the disease.

The first cases in Alberta of the influenza appeared on October 2, 1918, among a group of recently returned soldiers in Calgary. Within three weeks there were thousands of cases across the province and several deaths. The first case of flu in Red Deer was confirmed on October 25. Within a week dozens of others were reported. On October 28 the flu claimed its first victim, William Werner, a local farmer and father of eleven children.

In the meantime, public meetings were banned, church services were cancelled and the local schools, theatre and pool halls

In July 1918 Katherine Stinson became the first person to land an airplane at Red Deer. Her historic feat took place in front of the grandstand at the Red Deer Fair.

were ordered closed. The medical health officer, Dr. Henry George, ordered people to wear protective face masks. Those who failed to obey were charged by the police and fined by the courts. The homes of persons ill with the flu were quickly placed under quarantine and an isolation hospital was set up in the old Royal North West Mounted Police quarters on the west end of Victoria Avenue (43rd Street).

By early November over 200 people had fallen ill, including most of the boarders at St. Joseph's Convent and virtually all of the

On November 11, 1918, when official word of the end of the Great War was received, large crowds gathered on the City Square for ceremonies of celebration and thanksgiving.

staff and students at the Indian Industrial School. The number of serious cases grew so rapidly that the board of health rented the building next to the isolation hospital as a place for convalescing patients and as a temporary residence for the volunteer nurses, many of whom were local school teachers.

During the first week of November, the gloom of the epidemic was broken by the exciting news that an armistice was imminent. On November 7 the local CPR employees were given a half-day holiday on the rumour that such an agreement had already been signed. On November 8 the *Red Deer Advocate* printed two editions in order to keep up with the rapid succession of announcements and rumours.

On Monday, November 11, at 1:30 A.M., word was received in Red Deer that all hostilities would cease on all fronts at 11 a.m., London time. The *Red Deer Advocate* quickly printed a special issue with the news of the armistice, and the mayor declared a half-day public holiday. Plans were also quickly made for a civic celebration despite the board of health's injunction against any public gatherings.

At 12:30 P.M. all the bells and whistles in the city broke out in a thirty-minute peal of rejoicing. A large crowd of returned veterans, local dignitaries and ordinary citizens paraded through the streets and then gathered on the City Square for a ceremony of celebration and thanksgiving. There were numerous speeches and choruses of songs as well as a special playing on a gramophone of the federal minister of finance's Victory Loan speech. In the evening there was a giant bonfire in the City Square accompanied by the shooting of fireworks. The returned veterans were also treated to a special banquet sponsored by the city.

The joys over the end of the war were soon dampened by a renewed outbreak of the influenza which the medical health officer attributed to the peace celebrations. By the end of November the epidemic seemed to abate again; on December 4 the ban on public meetings was lifted. Church services recommenced and the Lyric Theatre reopened with the movie *The Ghost House*.

The flu lingered on and a number of new cases were reported over the following weeks. The schools were not reopened for another month and then had to be closed again when several students fell ill. All told, the epidemic claimed the lives of fourteen people in the city and another forty in the district. It was one more tragedy for the long-suffering people of Central Alberta.

As 1918 drew to a close the community began to face the aftermath of the most ter-

rible conflict in the history of civilization. A labour bureau was established to help find employment for returned soldiers. More than $180,000 were pledged in Central Alberta toward the latest Victory Loan campaign to raise the money needed to pay for war debts. Food shortages in Europe kept prices paid to farmers high, but rampant inflation continued to take a heavy toll on the local economy.

People began to discuss the most appropriate means of honouring the 114 young men of Red Deer and district who had given their lives in the Great War. Consideration was also given to ways of paying tribute to the more than 700 local veterans, many of whom were suffering from crippling wounds or broken health.

Throughout the war a number of plaques and scrolls had been unveiled in honour of those who had served and those who had died. As early as May 1917 city council had discussed erecting a special monument in the centre of the City Square. On December 16, 1918, the GWVA held a public meeting to consider a fitting and permanent memorial to those who had given their lives in the service of their country. While no firm decision was made, it was agreed that a fund should be organized to raise the money needed for such a memorial.

At its last meeting of 1918 city council considered presenting medals to the returning soldiers. Unfortunately, the mayor and the aldermen found that the cost of either silver or bronze medals was more than they felt the city could afford. Consequently, they decided to give special certificates of appreciation and remembrance. The financial crises of the war years were continuing to affect even the symbolic actions of the community.

The Great War had made a deep and lasting impact on the City of Red Deer and all of Central Alberta. It became the benchmark or division of time between the heady optimism of the pioneer boom years and the uncertain future of a postwar world. The era ahead was to be a time of peace. But all too often it also was to be a time of troubles.

LEFT: While the Red Deer Fire Brigade joined the victory parade to celebrate the end of the Great War, the men had to wear protective masks because of the terrible flu epidemic which had beset the community.

RIGHT: An unidentified soldier, one of hundreds of men who returned to Central Alberta at the end of the First World War suffering from wounds and uncertain about the future which awaited them.

Chapter 6

A Time of Peace, A Time of Troubles

LEFT: A view of Ross Street, looking west, taken just after the end of the First World War. The Alexandra Hotel on the right had closed in the aftermath of Prohibition.

ABOVE: City of Red Deer Treasury Bill, 1922.

For Red Deer and Central Alberta, the postwar era was a time of peace, but it was not a time of serenity. The incredible, adolescentlike optimism of the early part of the decade had been shattered by the tribulations of the later part. People were grateful that the great global conflict was finally over, but the new trials of inflation, unemployment, drought and recession tempered any hopes for a rosy future.

In mid-July 1919 the Red Deer Agricultural Society organized a Victory Fair to celebrate the end of the war and the new era of peace. The main attraction was Lieutenant George Gorman, a veteran pilot and former prisoner of war, who demonstrated a number of aeronautical feats and provided Red Deer's first passenger rides at $15 per flight. The other major attraction was a special Veterans' Day during which the mayor made the official presentations of the city's certificates of appreciation and remembrance. That event was capped in the evening by a mock battle which the *Red Deer Advocate* described as "quite realistic."

ABOVE: Following the Great War, airplanes became chief attractions at the Red Deer Fair.

BELOW: The expansion of the grain trade during the First World War persuaded companies to build new elevators in Red Deer.

The fair was an outstanding success and all previous attendance records were shattered. Unfortunately, there were a few disconcerting occurrences which marred the celebration. The opening ceremonies were delayed when a train wreck held up Brigadier General Macdonald, the officer commanding of Military District No. 13. A

bad forest fire in the west country made the air very smoky and big ashes fell constantly to the ground. The fair directors contended that the smoke only served to "cut off the full glare of the hot July sun."

The forest fire was a symptom of the return of the dry cycle of Central Alberta. The crop yields of 1918 were among the poorest on record, and those of 1919 were generally no better. Nevertheless, Central Alberta was more fortunate than many other parts of Western Canada. The parklands received more rain than the prairies to the south, and the resulting crops continued to fetch high prices. As the dry weather persisted, the people of Central Alberta were asked to contribute emergency relief supplies to the drought victims of Southern Alberta. Cattle from the dried-out districts were shipped north to the pastures east of Red Deer and around Pine Lake.

Throughout most of 1919 there was a modest amount of construction activity in the city. The tremendous increase in automobile ownership prompted the construction of two new garages. The marked shift to grain production during the war years persuaded the Alberta Pacific Grain Company and the Kenny Farm Agency to build new grain elevators. The new government-owned Canadian National Railroad took

W.J.Botterill 1st.V.P. — C.Sinclair. Sec.Treas. — J.B.Durand. 2nd.V.P.

W.Cookson. — W.G.Paterson. President. — P.W.Smith.

Officers G.W.V.A. Red Deer 1919

R.W.Alcock. — P.E.Kent.

R.C.P.Gee. — C.Roland.

In the aftermath of the war, the Great War Veterans Association became one of the chief supports for returned soldiers facing illness, economic hardships and, at times, loneliness.

over the bankrupt Canadian Northern and resumed the work on the branch line into Red Deer.

There was not, however, an appreciable increase in residential construction despite the numbers of returning veterans and newcomers to the city. As a consequence there was soon an acute shortage of housing in the community. There was also a sharp increase in school enrolment, which the local school systems found difficult to accommodate. The poor state of finances precluded the construction of either new schools or additions to existing ones.

During the First World War, the provincial government purchased the Alberta Ladies College from the Presbyterian Church. The government then used the facility as a sanatorium for veterans who had suffered terrible injuries to their minds during the war.

Ultimately, some interim solutions were found for the school problems. The Daughters of Wisdom of the separate school district were able to rent additional classroom and dormitory space in St. Mary's Apostolic School, as the Fathers of St. Mary of Tinchebray were no longer using the building for preseminary training. The public school board rented classroom space for $1,000 per year in the Anglican Parish Hall on Gaetz Avenue and Fifth Street North (55th Street). However, the Parish Hall required renovations in order to make it useable for school purposes, and the school board soon discovered that it was a very expensive building to heat.

This was no small consideration in the bitterly cold winter of 1919–1920. The first blizzard struck on October 8, and winter was not to release its grip again until the following May. Many farmers were unable to finish harvesting their crops. The feeding of livestock became very difficult as one heavy snowfall followed another.

The bleak weather matched the climate of the local economy. Rampant inflation continued to diminish the value of people's savings and incomes. The construction boomlet had petered out and unemployment became a widespread problem. The local Patriotic Fund Committee was empowered by the federal government to distribute emergency relief to veterans unable to work or unable to find work. Payments were only $50 per month for single men and $75 to $100 per month for families, but by spring more than $27,000 had been paid out by the committee. The GWVA also spent over $1,000 on special relief payments while the City of Red Deer disbursed several hundred dollars more to nonveterans.

Not surprisingly these grim economic conditions created a fair bit of labour unrest. Red Deer was largely a nonunion community, so most strikes and disruptions were organized by such province-wide groups as the railroad workers' unions. However, in January 1920 the staff at the

Soldiers' Sanitarium went on a wildcat strike over the discharge of one of their fellow workers. A few weeks later the local retail store employees organized an association and began to pursue their employers for better wages and working conditions. The city employees, while not formally organized, also pushed for improved salaries, which city council reluctantly granted early in 1920.

The reluctance of the city council stemmed from its continuing financial distress. Tax arrears continued to mount with the C & E Townsite Company being responsible for nearly 40 percent of the delinquent payments. The city tried to raise more revenue by hiking the mill rate and the business tax levy. It also tried to sell $90,000 in new ten-year treasury bills in an attempt to cover maturing bonds, ongoing expenses and the growing bank overdraft.

The sale was a disaster. For a month not a single bid was received. Finally, the mayor made a special trip to Eastern Canada to help sell the treasury bills. He had some success and $45,000 in bonds were sold. Meanwhile, the bank overdraft grew to more than $30,000, and the city was able to collect only 69 percent of the municipal taxes owing and 54 percent of the school tax levy.

Shortages of funds were not the only problems faced by the city. A sudden thaw in the last week of April 1920 caused extensive flooding in the downtown area. The mayor, several aldermen and a great many volunteers joined the city crews in the building of emergency dikes to control the floodwaters. The city also found itself inundated with forms from the provincial and federal governments demanding information on the community. One alderman suggested that it might be easier and cheaper to simply pay the fines for noncompliance.

Shortages of funds and declining enrolment finally prompted the Methodist Church to close the Indian Industrial School and move the remaining students to Edmonton. The school buildings and site were taken over by the Soldiers Settlement Board and used as an agricultural training centre for veterans.

By mid-1920 the economy took a slight turn for the better. The price of wheat rose to a postwar high as did prices for cattle and hogs. Alberta Government Telephones bought out the telephone system of the Western General for $85,000 and built a new telephone exchange building on Ross Street across from the City Square. This was a welcome development for the struggling Piper's Brickyard, which was given the contract to supply all the brick for the new structure.

The Soldiers Settlement Board in cooperation with the provincial government organized agricultural courses for veterans. These veterans were photographed in 1922 following one of the courses in a tent on the City Square.

While parades such as this one in 1919 on Gaetz Avenue continued to be held, the general mood in Red Deer was sombre as the community struggled with the severe postwar economic depression.

Unfortunately, it was to be the twenty-eight-year-old company's last major job.

In the late fall of 1920, the CNR finally finished laying the steel rails as far as the proposed station grounds on the corner of Ross Street and 3rd Avenue East (47th Avenue). The company announced that the ballasting of the track and construction of a station and freight shed would soon follow. Instead, the work ground to a halt. Farm prices were slumping badly, and the economy of Western Canada started to slide into one of the worst depressions in history.

The new hard times dealt a devastating blow to the community. As construction projects ceased, labourers were thrown out of work. As profits evaporated, businessmen laid off employees and went on a strictly cash basis to minimize bad debts. For many it did not help. Several businesses went bankrupt and others just quietly closed their doors. Some struggled on, but even the Western General, which many people viewed as a predatory monopoly, was unable to meet its payroll in October 1922.

The depth of the new economic distress is illustrated by an incident which occurred at the CPR station. A man from Penhold passed away, and through a mixup in communications, both of Red Deer's funeral homes were asked to arrange the funeral. When the two undertakers showed up to collect the body, a violent argument erupted. The man who lost the job had charges laid against his competitor. He had the small satisfaction of seeing the courts convict and fine the "successful" mortician.

The mood of economic desperation was particularly acute among the local farmers. The continuing dry cycle meant that crop yields were below average. Now, with the plunge in commodity prices, wheat was worth only one-third of what it had been in mid-1920. In the case of livestock, cattle and hogs netted only a few dollars if anything at all. Only the debts from the previous years remained high.

The farmers responded with radical political action. Traditional partisan loyalties had already been severely weakened during the war years. Now, the powerful United Farmers of Alberta (UFA) decided to become directly involved in politics. In the provincial election of July 1921, it swept to power with the Red Deer candidate, G.W. Smith, winning by more than 1,000 votes. In December Alfred Speakman of the UFA-backed Progressive Party won in the federal riding of Red Deer with nearly 70 percent of the vote. Unfortunately, electoral success did not bring immediate economic relief. In fact the passage in 1922 of new American tariffs against Canadian farm products only made matters worse.

The City of Red Deer found the economic hard times virtually impossible to manage. Tax arrears climbed to over $130,000. The city finally seized the property of its largest debtor, the C & E Townsite Company. However, this meant that $55,000 in tax arrears would never be paid. Meanwhile, unpaid bills grew by thousands of dollars and the bank overdraft soared.

The city desperately tried to raise its revenues. The property tax levy was raised to 46 mills and then to 65. The business tax rate was hiked to 20 percent from 12 percent. A new service tax was levied against nonratepayers, but the bylaw was badly worded and collections were poor. The aldermen even suggested the collection of rents from properties with tax arrears, but the city solicitor informed them that they could not legally do this.

The city also tried to slash expenditures. No grants were given to local societies and community groups except for a small payment toward the public librarian's salary. The mayor deflected some criticism by refusing to accept any of his salary. Nevertheless, the medical health officer quit in disgust, and the police chief later resigned for "personal and other reasons."

The financial crisis caused a marked strain in relations with the public school board. By law the city was required to pay all of the school district's requisition and not the amount actually collected. Moreover, the school board's budget, because of higher enrolments, had grown by one-third. The school district attempted to meet some of its financial shortfalls by borrowing money directly from the bank. It also unsuccessfully tried to levy a tax of $4 per year on all resident males over the age of twenty-one. In an attempt to improve relations with city council, the school trustees agreed to join the aldermen in a personal canvass of delinquent taxpayers.

It was the Memorial Hospital which suffered the worst from the economic crisis. Uncollected bills from patients skyrocketed and consequently so did the amount owed by the hospital to its suppliers and staff. An attempt was made to create a new tax-supported municipal hospital district encompassing the City of Red Deer and surrounding communities. The proposal was defeated in a plebiscite, largely by the farm vote.

Finally, the hospital went bankrupt when the City of Red Deer found itself unwilling and unable to advance any more money. The provincial government was forced to step in. Beds were closed, salaries were slashed and

staff were laid off. Other economy measures were taken. The hospital began to raise its own vegetables, and a dairy cow was purchased to supply milk and cream. The strain of the crises on the hospital's management was enormous. The nursing superintendent had two nervous breakdowns and finally had to resign her position.

While the Memorial hospital board, city council and the school boards were grappling with their financial quandaries, the community continued its work on the plans for a permanent memorial to those who had served and died in the Great War. The depression made fund-raising an enormous task. However, the impact of the war on the community had been so great that people were still willing to donate generously to such project.

Initially, there were three different proposals for the memorial. One was to construct a monument on a central site in the city. Another was to build a memorial community hall with a gym, swimming pool and auditorium. A third proposal was to purchase the old Alexandra Hotel and convert it into a recreation and community centre.

As the fund-raising campaign got under way, it became obvious that there was much more public support for a monument than for a community hall. When this decision

During the postwar economic depression, several municipalities, school boards and hospitals faced desperate financial problems. The Red Deer Memorial Hospital suffered the worst and was declared bankrupt by the provincial government.

could not assume the expense of a boulevard. The Memorial Committee decided to proceed as planned and to cover all the costs itself.

Meanwhile, the Memorial Committee decided that the monument should be in the form of a statue of the unknown soldier rather than a cobblestone pyramid or an obelisk. Major Frank Norbury, an architectural sculptor from the University of Alberta and a veteran of the Great War, was commissioned to carve the statue out of Tyndall limestone at a cost of $5050. The committee also chose to record the names of those who had served and those who had given their lives on two scrolls which were to be placed in a copper tube and deposited into the pedestal of the monument.

On September 15, 1922, the Cenotaph was officially unveiled by Lord Byng of Vimy, Governor General of Canada and a hero of the famous Battle of Vimy Ridge. An enormous crowd gathered for the ceremony. The local newspapers reported that the service of dedication and remembrance deeply moved all those who were present.

A prominent role was given at the Cenotaph ceremonies to the local militia which had been reactivated in Red Deer in 1921. Two units had been formed: the 78th Field Battery, Royal Canadian Artillery; and D

was reached, a new controversy erupted over where such a monument would be located. Some people, including the aldermen, wanted to have it placed on the City Square. However, a majority at a public meeting voted to have it located in the middle of Ross Street by the old land titles office building. City council announced that it

One of the most popular recreational activities of the early 1920s was golf. The sport, however, was controversial among those who objected to games being played on Sundays.

Company, First Alberta Regiment (31st Battalion). The battery initially used the old Empress Theatre on First Street North (51st Street) as its drill hall while the infantry company used the armoury. This caused some crowding problems for the GWVA, which had also been using the armoury since December 1918. Eventually, the GWVA was forced to move to an old store building on Ross Street in March 1924 although it was still allowed to use the armoury for its public dances.

Public dances at the armoury in the early 1920s were one of the leading forms of entertainment in the community. In 1921 the employees of AGT held a Valentine's Day dance which was such a resounding success that it became an annual event. Other groups such as the CPR employees organized similar affairs. Inevitably, there were some strong criticisms of these gatherings. The principal of the high school complained in 1922 that students were staying at the dances until the wee hours of the morning to the detriment of their studies.

There were other moral controversies in the community. In 1919 a local golf club was formed, and a number of citizens loudly objected to the playing of the sport on Sunday. One man wrote that "the public playing of golf on Sunday is a bad example

for the young people and will lead the boys into evil ways," while a local farmer complained of "the necessity of driving my family past Sunday golfers indulging themselves." The club members decided to ignore the protests and the organization continued to grow and prosper despite the economic hard times. In 1922 the club moved its course from West Park to the old Wilkins Ranch on the north side of the river. A large bungalow-style clubhouse was built, and arrangements were made to have a flock of sheep graze the course and keep the grass trimmed.

A more serious moral controversy concerned the illegal use of alcohol. In October 1920 the citizens of Red Deer had joined the majority of Albertans in voting for more stringent prohibition. However, these tougher laws failed to eliminate the use and abuse of liquor. There were cases in Red Deer involving fraudulent prescriptions of alcohol. One social establishment in the city was charged by the police with the selling of illegal beer. Illicit stills became a growing problem. In May 1922 an exasperated local magistrate declared that in the future he would gauge the severity of his sentences not on "the quantity of alcohol manufactured," but rather on the "quality of the liquor seized."

A program from one of the Rotary Club's first fund-raisers, which was staged with the help of the Red Deer Choral Society. In February 1923 Red Deer became the smallest community in Canada to form a Rotary Club.

Rotary Minstrel Show

REX THEATRE

◆━◂ ● ◂━◆

THURSDAY
APRIL 3rd
1924

at 8:30 sharp

◆━◂ ● ◂━◆

By the Members of the

RED DEER
ROTARY CLUB

R.B.

Mrs. Helen Moore Dawe .... Musical Director
Mrs. C. W. Sanders and Mrs. T. R. McDowell .... Violinists
Mrs. E. G. Johns .... Pianist
Miss Mona Ball, N. M. Burnett, J. M. Carscadden, F. Castle, H. B.
George, E. Galbraith, H. Lavender, V. Moore, G. W. Muir, J.
R. Weston, C. Collins, C. Weston, C. W. Long.

Finally, in November 1923 another province-wide plebiscite was held on whether to permit the consumption of beer in hotels and the sale of liquor in government outlets. Red Deer voted "dry" by a margin of 478 to 338, but the province as a whole voted "wet." Within a few months Red Deer had a government liquor outlet with a prominent officer in the local militia as the designated vendor.

While the politics of prohibition were changing, there were changes in the gender of politics and law as well. Women had been given the right to vote in provincial elections in 1916 and in federal elections in 1917. In 1921 Mrs. Laura Irish became the first woman in Red Deer to run for public office. She lost her bid to become a public school trustee by only ten votes. Five years later Mrs. Edith McCreight was successful in her bid to become Red Deer's first woman member of the public school board.

In 1921 the provincial government made it possible for women to be selected for jury duty. In November 1922 the Red Deer courthouse was the scene of the first court case in Canada to be heard by women jurors. The three women selected were Mrs. Jessie Huestis, Mrs. Zelma Smith and Mrs. Maude Horn. Unfortunately, the case was not without its complications. One potential juror refused to kiss the Bible as part of the juror's oath on the grounds that such a practice was unsanitary. The lawyer for the defendant tried to have the case overturned on the grounds that the sheriff had not served the clerk of the court with the proper papers. Since both offices were held by the same individual, the judge sarcastically asked if the lawyer wished to have the papers taken out of one pocket and placed in another.

Red Deer also had long been a progressive community in its appreciation of natural history. For over fifteen years the city had been the headquarters of one of the province's leading naturalist organizations, the Alberta Natural History Society (ANHS). In 1922 the ANHS persuaded J.J. Gaetz to have a wilderness area he owned around two oxbow lakes declared a Dominion Bird Sanctuary. While this designation did not provide as much protection for the wildlife and their habitat as the Society had hoped, it was one of the first attempts to save the native parkland rather than to develop it.

One of the key figures in the ANHS had been Dr. Henry George. Since 1907 he had operated a small museum on the corner of Ross Street and Second Avenue East (48th Avenue). In 1922 ill health forced Dr. George to move to British Columbia. The city found itself financially unable to take over the museum's operation, and the provincial government was uninterested. As a result the collections of artifacts were either sold or donated away, and Red Deer lost one of its cultural institutions.

Red Deer lost its museum, but it did

acquire a new post office facility in 1922. While it was not the new structure which had been promised, particularly at election times, since 1913, the renovated land titles office building was still a great improvement over the former cramped quarters in the News Block on Gaetz Avenue.

The summer of 1922 saw two other welcome developments. The CNR finally finished the work on its branch line into the city, and after the station was built in the early fall, passenger service on the line was commenced. As well, the provincial government built the East Bridge across the Red Deer River to the Joffre district. This new transportation link served to greatly enhance the agricultural trading area of the city.

By 1923 the economy of Red Deer and Central Alberta slowly began to improve. Tax collections increased, and the city was able to avoid borrowing any short-term funds from the bank until the late fall. In the case of the Memorial Hospital, the financial corner was finally turned, and another attempt was made to create a municipal hospital district. When the rural areas once again rejected the proposal, the provincial government decided to create a new district covering only the City of Red Deer. The hospital's assets and property were transferred to a new board and $10,000 was paid to the city for its equity. A new revenue structure was set up with a three mill property tax levy, a six dollar per annum charge for nonratepayers, a one dollar per day patient fee for taxpayers and much higher rates for nonresidents. The scheme, which formally came into effect in April 1923, worked very well. The Red Deer Municipal Hospital soon became a model for other urban communities in the province.

The improved outlook for the local businessmen was reflected in February 1923 with the chartering of the city's first service club, the Rotary Club. At the time, Red Deer was the smallest urban centre in Canada to have a branch of that international business and

A group of emigrants boarding a ship in Scotland on their way to Red Deer. In 1923 large numbers of settlers were brought to Central Alberta from the Hebrides by the Scottish Immigrant Aid Society.

professional organization. One of the club's first major projects was the installation of playground equipment on the City Square. Over 600 children turned out for the official opening ceremonies in May 1924.

The outlook for the local farmers received a major boost in the summer of 1923 with the organization of the Alberta Wheat Pool. The intention of this marketing cooperative was to give farmers much more clout in the selling of their grain. The farmers of Central Alberta reacted to the concept so enthusiastically that over 6,000 signed up for the pool within a few weeks. The results seemed impressive. Within a year the price of wheat rose by nearly 60 percent.

The spirit of cooperative action quickly spread to other sectors in the agricultural community. In the spring of 1924 the Farmers Cooperative Marketing Association took over the marketing of eggs in Red Deer and area. At the same time the Central Alberta Dairy Pool was formed at Alix, and a number of Red Deer area dairymen decided to join the organization.

While the established farmers were busy organizing cooperatives, there was a new influx of potential settlers to the region. Many of these newcomers were brought over from the Hebrides of Scotland by the

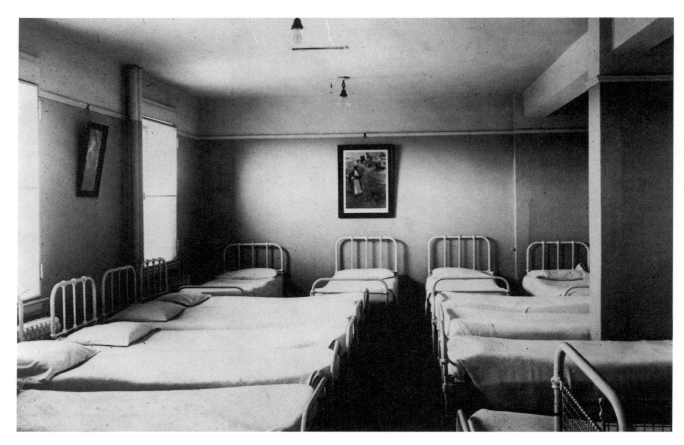

In 1923 the provincial government decided to turn the Soldiers Sanatorium into an institution for the residential care and training of mentally handicapped children. The new Provincial Training School was soon full.

Scottish Immigrant Aid Society. Some fifty families arrived in Red Deer in May 1923, and while arrangements were made to find farms for them, temporary accommodations were provided at the old Indian Industrial School. Over the next year several more families arrived in Red Deer and were resettled in Central Alberta or other parts of the province.

This flurry of new immigrants and the improved economy helped to restore a new sense of optimism. The CPR decided to make improvements to its rail yards, including the construction of new coal chutes and a new coking plant. Scott Fruit Company opened a new wholesale outlet on Gaetz Avenue and the Atlas Lumber Company began operations in the city.

The new sense of confidence and hope prompted the public school board to draw up plans for a new high school building. Although such a structure was greatly needed because of overcrowded classrooms and the decrepit state of the 1894 schoolhouse,

the ratepayers were not as enthusiastic about the proposal as the board. The project was defeated in a plebiscite in August 1924 by a vote of 245 to 79.

Red Deer did acquire a new type of school in 1923. The provincial government decided to close the Soldiers' Sanitarium and establish in its place a centre for the residential care and training of mentally handicapped children. This new institution, known as the Provincial Training School, was the only one of its kind in the province and was consequently soon full to capacity. The medical superintendent recommended the construction of additional buildings to supplement the accommodations in the former Alberta Ladies College building. Like the ratepayers of the public school district, the Provincial government did not see that the needs outweighed the costs. Therefore, nothing was done for several more years.

Another type of facility which many in the community felt was seriously needed was an arena. Red Deer had been without such a place since the roof collapsed on the old skating rink in the winter of 1907. City council did not feel that its financial position had improved enough to build an arena with public funds. A community-based fund-raising effort was launched instead, and a nonprofit joint-stock company was formed to solicit contributions. The project was given a big boost when $4000 was donated by the newly formed Elks Club and the local Rotary Club. By the early fall of 1925 enough money had been raised to start construction on the block east of the City Square. Work proceeded quickly, and the building was officially opened with an elaborate ice carnival on December 15, 1925.

The new tin-covered arena proved to be a tremendous boon to local winter sports. In the season following the opening of the facility, the Red Deer Hockey Club won the 1925–26 Provincial Intermediate championship. It was the first sports team in the history of the city to attain such an honour. Red Deer also had a tradition of fine women's hockey teams. Within a few years of the construction of the covered rink, the Amazons became provincial champions twice.

Although city council felt that it lacked the means to build the new arena, it determined that the time had come to tackle the long-standing problem of the city's utilities and the Western General Electric company. Negotiations to purchase the electrical system were commenced with a considerable amount of hot public debate. The city's initial offer of $51,000 was rejected by the company largely because it felt that it should be compensated for new steam boilers which it had purchased but not yet installed. The city then appealed to the provincial government for help, and the dispute was referred to the board of public utility commissioners for arbitration. In September 1925 the board ruled that a fair value for the company's plant and assets would be $74,000, including $23,000 for the steam boilers.

During the 1920s and 1930s, Red Deer had an outstanding women's hockey team, the Amazons. Pictured here are Scotty Lee, Audrey Stephenson, Evelyn Nichols, Ernie Wells, Lois Botterill, Babe Thompson, Helen Hayhoe, Vera Houston, Dorothy Kitching and Irene Dell.

The utilities board also recommended that the existing system be upgraded to comply with the Electrical Protection Act and that new street lighting be installed. With these recommendations in mind, the city submitted a bylaw in the amount of $85,000 to the ratepayers for ratification. The vote of approval was nearly unanimous. Arrangements were then made to sell the debentures needed to finance the purchase and to make the required amendments to the city's charter. On April 1, 1926, everything was completed and the city took over the operation of the electrical utility.

The former managing director of the Western General claimed that the city's staff lacked the competence to profitably run the plant and distribution system. His warnings proved to be unfounded. In the first six months of city management, the utility turned a profit of over $1,000. In the following year the operating surplus amounted to several thousands of dollars. Instead of being a terrible financial burden, the purchase of the Western General proved to be a lucrative means of solving the city's economic problems.

By the latter part of the 1920s, the city's financial status had greatly improved. Tax collections continued to increase and by late 1926, the bank overdraft had been wiped

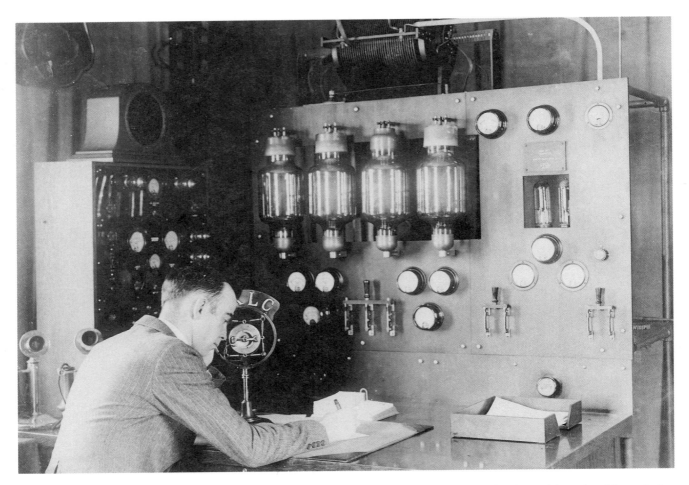

In 1927 the Alberta Pacific Grain Company started Red Deer's first radio station, CKLC. While most programs originated out of Calgary, local announcers such as Charles Wood did make some broadcasts from the studio on the South Hill.

out. The strict "pay-as-you-go" policy which had been adopted several years before meant that there was usually an excess of revenue over expenditures. This allowed the city to pay off a significant portion of its debenture and treasury bill debt, a process which was accelerated with the new revenues from the utilities.

The wonderful situation became even better in 1928 when the city signed a long-term contract with Calgary Power Ltd. to purchase hydroelectric power on a wholesale basis. This new agreement provided electricity at a fraction of the cost of generation at the old Western General steam plant. Moreover, as the distribution system was still owned and operated by the municipality, the city was able to continue reaping the profits of retailing the power. The electrical utility had become a veritable bonanza, and within a short period of time, the city was virtually its own banker.

Meanwhile, the public school board also enjoyed a significant improvement in its fiscal position. The board was able to grant modest pay raises to its staff in 1927 and to pay for a number of renovations to the school buildings. Overcrowding remained a serious problem, and the assembly hall in the 1907 schoolhouse had to be used for classes after the termination of the lease of the Parish Hall in 1925. The city council chamber was rented for extra classroom space in 1927, but this proved to be a rather unsatisfactory arrangement.

Finally, the public school board decided to again propose the construction of a new high school. This time the ratepayers agreed to the $60,000 project. Construction work began in the summer of 1928. After classes were moved to the new schoolhouse in December, the old 1894 building was demolished.

The separate school board also enjoyed

In 1928 the Red Deer Public School Board built a new high school to replace the 1894 schoolhouse, which was literally starting to collapse.

some improvement to its school facilities. The Daughters of Wisdom were able to purchase the St. Mary's Apostolic School building for $700 in 1925. In 1928 a large addition was constructed on the north side of the building to provide extra dormitory and classroom space. Unfortunately for the sisters, they continued to receive only $200 a year for all the school accommodation they provided.

While conditions for city council and the school boards improved, there were some modest developments in the business sector as well. The National Grain Company built an elevator next to the CNR station in 1925, a new flour mill was constructed on Gaetz Avenue North in 1926 and a new creamery was built on First Street South (49th Street) in 1927. It was also in 1927 that the Alberta Pacific Grain Company established Red Deer's first radio station, CKLC. A small building and tower were erected near the hospital on the South Hill, but most of the transmissions consisted of grain price reports from the parent company and rebroadcasts of programs originating at a station in Calgary.

In 1928 another grain elevator was built by the Alberta Wheat Pool, and the T. Eaton Company became the first national department store in Red Deer when it pur-

chased W.E. Lord's retail establishment. As might have been expected, given the continuing growth in automobile ownership, two more garages were built.

There were a number of other developments in the community. In 1925 the Roman Catholics built a new church, Sacred Heart, on Fifth Street North (55th Street) and the Nazarenes started a Bible camp in the Woodlea area of the city. In 1927 the Nazarene Church started a religious school in temporary quarters in a house on Second Street South (48th Street), and after two years they began construction of a Bible college on Gaetz Avenue South.

In October 1925 a fire seriously damaged Red Deer's movie theatre, and a few weeks later the old Empress Theatre reopened. In 1926 the Empress's owners, the Beatty Brothers, built a new 485-seat theatre on Ross Street, which they named the Crescent. When sound equipment was installed three years later, the people of Red Deer were able to enjoy their first "talking" movies.

There were, however, a few setbacks in those years as well. The CNR finally announced that its rail line would not be extended beyond the city, but rather would remain essentially a spur off of the main branch to Nordegg. The *Red Deer News,* which had been struggling for many years,

ABOVE: The business district along Gaetz Avenue, north from 2nd Street South (48th Street). By the late 1920s Red Deer had become a relatively prosperous, typical prairie town.

RIGHT: During the 1920s and 1930s, high school amateur theatrical productions became a popular form of entertainment.

ceased publication in 1926, and its assets were purchased by the *Red Deer Advocate*.

Basically, Red Deer changed very little throughout most of the decade. The return of a wetter climate after 1924 and improved agricultural prices brought a measure of prosperity to the community. Still, Red Deer's population in 1926 was somewhat smaller than it had been in 1921, and by the end of the 1920s there were only sixteen more residents in the city than there had been ten years before.

As the so-called Roaring Twenties came to an end, Red Deer was just entering its strongest boom in more than sixteen years. Nearly a quarter of a million dollars in con-

With the onset of the Great Depression and a pending election, the provincial government built a new court house in Red Deer as a job creation project.

struction projects had been started, including the Nazarene's Northern Bible College, new buildings at the Provincial Training School, the Safeway grocery store, four new business blocks, additions to two lumberyards, another service station and several new houses. The provincial government began to look seriously at constructing the long-promised court house building, while AGT overhauled its telephone system so that it could install automatic telephones in early 1930.

The most exciting news came in May 1929 when the E.B. Eddy Company announced plans to build a match factory in Red Deer. The company estimated that as many as 100 people would be employed in the plant. The townspeople were so enthused at the prospects of the venture that the financial concessions granted by city council to the company were ratified with the first unanimous bylaw vote in the city's history.

Unfortunately for the E.B. Eddy project and for Red Deer's nascent boom, the financial markets of Eastern Canada and the United States abruptly crashed in October 1929. The global economy began to slide precipitously into a deep and terrible depression, and a new time of troubles descended upon the world.

For a brief period Red Deer seemed to be able to resist the coming tide of misfortune. Agricultural prices recovered from the dramatic drops of October. By January 1930 they were only slightly below what they had been three months before. The numerous construction projects commenced in Red Deer in 1929 continued on into the early months of 1930. The provincial government, which faced a general election in the spring, rushed the court house project forward, thereby creating new construction jobs.

In January 1930 the city council decided to share some of the profits of its lucrative utilities system with the local citizens. Light and power rates were substantially reduced, but this did not hurt the city's revenues as there was subsequently a major increase in consumption. In February the city council cut the mill rate by 9 percent, but with the lower burden on the ratepayers, there was a compensating improvement in the rate of tax collections.

As the year progressed, however, the vice of the depression began to tighten. Farm prices dropped dramatically. Within a few months the price of grain was only one-third of what it had been at the start of the year. As local farmers stopped buying, local merchants saw their profits suddenly evaporate. A wave of business closures and bankruptcies soon followed. As the construction

City Hall Park, c 1931. While the City of Red Deer faced hard times in the 1930s, it did relatively better than some other communities because local farmers were never dried out and because the city was debt-free.

projects of 1929 came to an end, there were few new ones to fill the void and unemployment began to mount. Conditions became so grim so quickly that a local bank was forced to borrow $3 from a customer one evening when the man who had been cleaning the offices "was not prepared to extend credit on his account in the present business and financial situations."

Paradoxically, as the economy plunged downward, the attention of the community turned to aviation. A flying club was formed in early 1930. In April, with the help of the local board of trade, it leased a site along the Calgary–Edmonton Trail for an airstrip. The new airfield was finished within six weeks and officially opened on May 24 with a spectacular air circus that attracted more than 5,000 people.

Shortly thereafter the Federal Department of Aviation made arrangements to use the new airport as an emergency landing field for the air mail flights between Calgary and Edmonton. The federal authorities also built a radio beacon on a site along Gaetz Avenue, just south of the city limits. A commercial aviation company, Central United Airways, commenced operations at the airport and provided both passenger flights and student instruction. Unfortunately, the problems engendered by the economic

depression proved to be too much for the new venture, and the company soon quietly went out of business.

Meanwhile, the City of Red Deer tried to grapple with the burgeoning unemployment problem. A new concrete traffic bridge was built across Waskasoo Creek on Ross Street East as a public works project, but the worksite was besieged by a hoard of men seeking work. City council set a policy of hiring local residents over transients, but there were still more applicants than there were jobs. In the fall the city entered a joint unemployment relief scheme with the provincial government and began an extensive program of grading and gravelling streets. Although the wages were only forty cent an hour, the $7,500 budget was exhausted by February and the project was discontinued.

While the economic climate was becoming increasingly bleak, the winter of 1930–31 was one of the mildest on record. Even in January the temperatures were generally above freezing and there was virtually no snow. Paradoxically, the pleasant conditions caused some aggravations. For example, when the local Welliver rink won the provincial curling championships at a bonspiel in the city in early March, the deciding games had to be played between midnight

The sanctuary of Gaetz United Church in the early 1930s. Churches and local organizations such as the Service To Others group joined municipal officials in trying to alleviate some of the distress of the Great Depression.

and 9:30 A.M., when the temperatures were cooler and the ice conditions were somewhat better. The long dry spell also caused some serious problems. On March 3, 1931, a strong wind created a terrible dust storm that brought darkness to the city in the middle of the afternoon. Forest and brush fires broke out and caused widespread damage, particularly in the areas west of Red Deer.

The drought finally came to an end in the late spring. On June 16 a sudden rainstorm dumped over four centimetres of rain on the city in twenty minutes. Basements were flooded, roofs were damaged and cars stalled when their distributors got wet. The city's sewer system was unable to manage the immense runoff, thereby causing some serious sanitary problems for the townspeople.

While the cloudburst may have caused some temporary hygienic problems, the health care of the community received a tremendous boost in June 1931 with the formation of the Red Deer Full-Time Health Unit. This community health service was a joint proposal of the Rockefeller Foundation and the provincial government with the Red Deer and district unit being one of two pilot projects in the province. Despite the severity of the Depression, the benefits of such a health promotion organization were

very obvious to the municipal councils in the region. With the Rockefeller Foundation and the provincial government agreeing to pick up 75 percent of the $10,000 annual cost, the local authorities gave the project their unanimous backing.

There were a few other bright spots for the community. The new court house was finished and opened with elaborate ceremony in March 1931. The city council felt that its financial position remained strong enough that it lowered business taxes by 20 percent and property taxes by one mill. The National Fence Company, a subsidiary of the Phoenix Lumber Company, built a new $15,000 plant in the city, and the Dench Cartage Company opened a distributing warehouse on Gaetz Avenue North. The 40th Annual Fair was a tremendous success, partly because pari-mutuel betting was allowed on the horse races for the first time.

Conditions quickly turned very grim again. The price of wheat plunged by over 25 percent in the late summer, and there were heavy layoffs of staff by the CPR. The new fence factory was completed, but it remained largely idle because of a lack of orders. People began to despair about the coming winter.

New schemes for handling the unemployment problem were devised by the

HOW TO TELL A KLANSMAN

He is a white man.

He is a Protestant.

He is a Gentile.

He is a Christian.

He ~~is native born.~~

He is a loyal Canadian.

He swears his Allegiance to the British Empire, not to the Pope.

He believes in freedom of worship and hates nobody.

He opposes Political Rome, not Religious Rome.

He will not permit Roman Catholics and others to proscribe him.

He claims the same right to organize that he grants to Roman Catholics and others.

He upholds Public Schools.

He is a law abiding citizen.

He upholds virtuous womanhood.

He opposes trash immigration.

He defends the Canadian Home.

He believes Yellow Supremacy is O.K. for Japan, Black Supremacy O.K. for Africa and stands unalterably for White Supremacy in Canada.

He stands for Canada for the Canadians and the British.

He believes in klanishness among his kind as Jews and others practice it among their kind.

He believes there is no neutral position.

He has the courage to back these convictions, and the nerve to get in now and not wait until the work is all done.

BY A KLANSMAN

A Ku Klux Klan pamphlet from Red Deer in the early 1930s. The line "He is native born" was crossed out because the possessor of the pamphlet had been born in England.

provincial and federal governments. Major roads were to be built as public works projects, and relief camps were established west of Rocky Mountain House. In Red Deer the city's share of unemployment relief projects was reduced to 25 percent from 50 percent, and the grant from the senior governments was doubled to $15,000. A new water reservoir was built on the northeast corner of Michener Hill, and work resumed on the grading and gravelling of streets.

In October 1931 a new organization, the Service To Others Club, was formed to help the Central Welfare Board in its work with the destitute. In December a National Emergency Relief Appeal Committee was established to raise funds to supplement government relief payments. The local campaign objective was set at $1,500 and incredibly, given the general economic conditions, nearly $1,800 was raised.

The funds were sorely needed. The direct relief rates paid by the city were only $4 per week for a man and wife, and 50 cents to $1 for each child. The premise was that these were only temporary payments which would cover the cost of groceries. Gradually, it became evident that the unemployment problem was not a temporary one and that consideration had to be given to other expenses such as fuel, rent and clothing. Still,

there were some who complained about the "idle relief recipients" who "hung around the poolrooms" and "wasted the taxpayer's money."

Meanwhile, the ugly spectre of bigotry and religious intolerance reared its head in Red Deer. For two or three years there had been a small branch of the Ku Klux Klan in the area, and in May 1930 a tar-and-feathering incident at Blackfalds was blamed on a small group of alleged Klansmen. In June 1931 a Klan organizer, J.J. Maloney, held a half-dozen public meetings in Central Alberta. They were frighteningly successful. Several hundred people attended, and although many were more curious than committed, the local Klan organization became stronger and bolder. It launched a series of public denunciations of "moral transgressions" in the community, and a cross was burned on the brow of the North Hill.

Within a year the storm abated almost as quickly as it had surged. Many people were offended by the strident and intolerant positions of the Klan. As well, the Klan was supposed to be a secret society, but in a small community like Red Deer, very little remained secret for very long. The faults and foibles of the organization became public knowledge and rumours of ridicule began to circulate. One widespread story was that a prominent Klansman had been forced to quit because his wife would not let him use the bed sheets. Whatever the reasons the Klan's membership ebbed and the attention of the community soon returned to the deepening depression.

By 1932 economic conditions had hit bottom. The price of wheat plunged to twenty-one cents a bushel, while barley sank to ten cents a bushel. Prices for livestock fell so sharply that a number of farmers found that the sales of their animals fetched less than the costs of shipping them to market. In the city more businesses went bankrupt and the rate of unemployment rose even higher. The *Red Deer Advocate* began running full-page ads pleading with people to do everything possible to provide more jobs.

The increased severity of the Depression dealt many blows. The radio beacon on Gaetz Avenue South was closed by the federal government as an economy measure. The provincial government disbanded the Alberta Provincial Police Force and their duties in Red Deer were taken over by the Royal Canadian Mounted Police. The provincial government also cut back its grants to municipalities, school boards and organizations such as the Red Deer Agricultural Society (Fair Board).

The public school board, the hospital board and city council reduced the salaries they paid as did virtually all the businesses in the city. Even the wages paid on unemployment relief projects were cut from forty cents per hour to thirty cents. The Provincial Director of Charity and Relief recommended to city council that the rates be further reduced to either twenty-five cents per hour or one dollar per day.

In January 1933 the Board of Trade slashed its fees by 50 percent in order to maintain its membership, and other groups such as the Red Deer Aero Club folded. In May 1933 radio station CKLC ceased operations, and the facility on the South Hill was dismantled.

Ever since the start of the Depression, a great many transients had been travelling through Red Deer looking for work. Now their numbers reached staggering proportions. The police chief estimated that as many as 150 unemployed men were passing through the city a day. There were no jobs for them; there were not enough jobs for those living in the community. Many of the transients still went from door to door to see if there might be some small chore or household task they could do. The townspeople often responded by at least providing them with something to eat.

Many of the job-seekers arrived in Red Deer as hitchhikers on freight trains.

Inevitably, there were several tragic accidents as the men jumped off or climbed onto the moving boxcars. The worst accident occurred in North Red Deer in June 1933 when three exhausted young men from Regina fell asleep on the tracks and were run over by a freight train.

The railroad companies periodically tried to clear the transients from their trains and property. The city police did their utmost to ensure that these wandering jobless men did not linger in the community. Until they moved on, many of the men camped in a "hobo jungle" in the willow brush along the railroad tracks on the southern edge of the city. Some, particularly in cold weather, were allowed to spend the night in the police station and in the morning were given a meal if they were leaving the city. In October 1932 the mayor reported that well over 500 transients had been accommodated by the city in the preceding four weeks.

Part of the reason why so many men flocked to the Red Deer district was the fact that while conditions were extremely grim, they were still relatively better than the situations in other parts of Alberta and Western Canada. Central Alberta never experienced the dust bowl conditions of the prairies to the south, and the local farmers were always able to harvest a crop. As a result, throughout the Depression, the residents of Red Deer and area were able to ship carloads of donated food and emergency relief supplies to dried-out communities in Southern Saskatchewan.

Moreover, the City of Red Deer remained in much better financial shape than most other cities and towns. The publicly owned utilities provided a steady income, and because the city had been aggressively reducing its debt load since the early 1920s, money which would have otherwise been spent on interest payments was available for operational expenses and relief projects.

The city council continued its policy of keeping expenditures to an absolute mini-

In 1934 the newly formed Central Alberta Pioneers and Old Timers Association held its first annual banquet and roundup at the Elks Hall.

mum and of paying off debentures and treasury bills whenever possible. It also cut property taxes every year and was therefore able to provide some assistance to the local ratepayers. With so many other municipal governments defaulting on their bonds or raising their taxes to astonishing levels, Red Deer soon became renowned as an "economic miracle." Government officials and financiers flooded the city administration with requests for information on how the city was managing to accomplish such wonders. Ironically, many investors also wrote to offer to lend the city money as its credit rating was so good.

By late 1933 the economic situation improved slightly. Farm prices rose a bit and the city had one of the best tax collections in years. Relief rates were raised to $20 a month for a man and wife, plus an additional $2 for each dependent child. The city even gained a new business when MacDonald's Consolidated opened a grocery warehouse on Gaetz Avenue North. Conditions were still dreadful, but at least they had improved.

In 1934 the community began to turn its attention to its history. Fifty years had passed since settlement started in Central Alberta, and the young pioneers were now becoming senior citizens. There may have been another reason for the nostalgia. With all the suffering of the Depression, the heady boom times of the settlement era must have looked even better. If there was not much to celebrate in the present, then one could at least celebrate the past.

In January 1934 the Red Deer and Central Alberta Old Timers Association was formed with Tom Gaetz as the first president. In March the association's first reunion or roundup was held at the Elks Hall. In April another successful banquet was organized by the Board of Trade to honour Raymond Gaetz, the first mayor of the Town of Red Deer. In late June the Old Timers' Association and the board of trade jointly sponsored a large picnic at the original settlement site at the Old Crossing.

The largest celebration was planned for

July in conjunction with the annual Red Deer Fair. The event was dubbed the Golden Jubilee in recognition of the fiftieth anniversary of Reverend Leonard Gaetz taking the first homestead on the current townsite of Red Deer. The jubilee surpassed all expectations. The special parade on the opening day extended for over a kilometre. Between five and six thousand people flocked to the fairgrounds for each of the three days of the reunion and fair. A large buffalo barbecue was a highlight of the special pioneers' banquet.

The *Red Deer Advocate* marked the historic occasion by publishing a special forty-eight page souvenir edition, which included extensive write-ups on the growth and development of the city and district. The newspaper also printed a booklet of reminiscences written by the first mayor of the city, F.W. Galbraith, prior to his death in 1934. The history of the community was finally being recorded.

In the fall of 1934 the Old Timer's Asso-ciation purchased two and one-half hectares of land at the Old Crossing from the CPR and the Municipal District of Pine Lake for $21. The plan was to use the property for reunions and picnics and to preserve its historical character for future generations.

As the year drew to a close the feelings of bitterness and despair over the long Depression began to well up again. For many months a new monetary theory, Social Credit, had been advocated as a solution to the economic hard times by William Aberhart, a popular Calgary school principal and evangelist. The UFA government had trouble with the complex theory, which Stephen Leacock had described as "certain profundities of a British fog made understandable in sunny Alberta by the force of prayer." However, when the UFA legislators rejected the concept, the angry supporters of Social Credit decided to take direct political action and contest the next provincial election.

Few predicted the outcome. In August 1935 the Social Credit movement swept to

The construction of the new Central Alberta Dairy Pool Condensery on Gaetz Avenue in 1936 brought great excitement to the community as it meant new jobs and new industry for Red Deer.

Marjorie Wood with the archery set made by her husband, Kerry Wood, for presentation to Lord Tweedsmuir, Governor General of Canada, when he visited Red Deer in 1937.

power and all the UFA members of the legislature were defeated. The Red Deer riding, which had already elected an opposition party candidate in a by-election in November 1931, joined the rest of the province in the overwhelming vote for the new economic panacea. In the federal election which followed, the Social Credit candidate, Eric Poole, was elected as Red Deer's Member of Parliament by a massive majority.

Unfortunately, as had been the case with the farmers' political revolt in 1921, electoral success did not bring immediate relief. Still there were a few bright spots for Red Deer. The city was able to collect almost all of the 1935 tax levy. In April 1936, when Alberta became the first province in Canada to default on its bonds, the City of Red Deer was able to pay off the last of its treasury bills. In June 1936 the public school board

was able to raise some teachers' salaries, and a few months later city council restored most of the salary cuts it had made in 1932.

The most exciting news came in March 1936 when the Central Alberta Dairy Pool announced its plans to build a $100,000 milk condensery on Gaetz Avenue North. This new plant provided a large number of construction jobs and also gave a big boost to the local dairy farmers. Its importance to the region was demonstrated when nearly 5,000 people turned out on September 5 to watch Premier Aberhart and Trade and Industry Minister Ernest Manning officially open the facility.

If the construction of the CADP condensery was the happiest news of 1936, perhaps the saddest was the passing of King George V on January 20 after a reign of over twenty-five years. Another shock came in December when King Edward VIII suddenly abdicated the throne so that he could marry an American divorcee. When the new monarch, King George VI, was crowned on May 12, 1937, the whole city joined in a festive celebration. A large parade was held as were devotional services and a patriotic gathering on the City Square. One highlight of the day was the planting of commemorative trees in the park on Ross Street East, which has henceforth been known as Coronation Park.

Two months after the coronation, the Governor General of Canada, Lord Tweedsmuir, visited Red Deer. Unlike the Earl of Bessborough's brief stop in the city in September 1932, this vice-regal visit was to last three days and include trips to several other local communities. Although Central Alberta had been experiencing one of the driest springs and summers in its history, heavy rains began the day before the Governor General's arrival. During his stay nearly fifteen centimetres of precipitation fell. Consequently, most of the scheduled events were cancelled. However, Lord Tweedsmuir commented that if he had known that his visit would have ended the drought so dramatically, he would have come much earlier.

While the heavy rains may have ruined one of the more important social events in the city, they also indicated that the great dry cycle of the early 1930s was starting to come to an end. As a result the farmers of Central Alberta began to enjoy better crop yields, and with farm prices generally edging upward, prosperity was slowly returning to the Central Alberta parklands.

The better times manifested themselves in some rather modest and mundane ways. The public school board, after much debate, decided to spend $600 on a 16mm movie projector. All of the old wooden water mains were finally replaced by the city with cast iron ones, and regular household garbage collection was commenced. City council agreed to contribute financially to the improvement of the swimming hole in North Red Deer as many youngsters from the southside were using it. As well, although the aldermen felt that they could

not afford to buy an automobile for the police department, they were in favour of making arrangements to use taxicabs in cases of emergency.

A few other developments were more significant. In 1937 the Red Deer Mutual Telephone Company, a cooperative venture, took over AGT's rural lines and provided telephone service to the farmers in the Red Deer district. Three new business blocks were built and several others were renovated and expanded. In the fall, construction began on a 250 barrel-a-day oil refinery just south of the city limits.

A sense of optimism slowly began to emerge. Several new organizations were formed. A young men's section of the board of trade was created, and a professional and business women's group, the Quota Club, became active. In May 1937 a local Kinsmen Club was chartered, and the following year the Red Deer Lions Club was organized.

Although prosperity was beginning to seep back into the local economy and a

The official opening of the reconstructed Fort Normandeau by the Central Alberta Pioneers and Old Timers Association at the old Red Deer Crossing on July 1, 1938.

sense of optimism was developing among some of the younger members of the community, the political turmoil and backlash continued. Social Credit had not brought the immediate and dramatic turnaround that many people had expected. An insurgency movement broke out among several Social Credit MLAs, including the representative from Red Deer.

The rebel MLAs were somewhat mollified when the government introduced a number of radical pieces of legislation. To some people, however, the actions were still not enough. They bitterly pointed to the continuing high levels of unemployment and farm bankruptcies and reminded the Government that it had not fulfilled its promise to pay a $25 a month "dividend." To others the measures were too much. They saw the monetary reforms and debt readjustments as being tantamount to the confiscation of private property.

Feelings ran very high. A public meeting held in Red Deer in July 1938, with the Provincial Treasurer as the featured speaker, broke up in violent disorder. There were howls of outrage when the federal government disallowed some pieces of legislation and the courts declared others to be *ultra vires*. A powerful anti-Social Credit "Unity" movement was formed in Red Deer in late 1938 and plans were made to contest the next provincial election.

Despite the political tumult, economic conditions continued to improve in Red Deer and Central Alberta. In 1938 a large new department store was constructed on Gaetz Avenue and another movie theatre, the Capitol, was built on Ross Street. The federal government proceeded with the construction of a new airport between Red Deer and Penhold and the radio beacon on Gaetz Avenue South was reactivated.

One unique construction project came when the Old Timers' Association decided to rebuild a portion of old Fort Normandeau. The main floor of the barracks building (i.e. the old stopping house) was hauled

Gaetz Avenue South in 1939, showing the newly constructed Eaton's Store.

back to the Old Crossing from a neighbouring farm and the original logs were either repaired or replaced. The structure was officially opened with a large picnic on Dominion Day 1938.

In 1939 an astonishing $300,000 worth of building projects were started, including a large new hotel, a new Eaton's store, a water filtration plant, a new wing of the Municipal Hospital, additional buildings at the Provincial Training School, three new business blocks, a number of garages and service stations and several new residences. After ten long and often desperate years, it looked like boom times were finally returning to Red Deer.

There was a particular note of excitement in the spring of 1939 when King George VI and his wife, Queen Elizabeth, visited Alberta. For weeks the newspapers were full of articles on the impending visit and on the Royal Family. On June 2, when Their Majesties stopped at Edmonton, it was estimated that over one-half of the

total population of Red Deer journeyed to try to catch a glimpse of them. It was perhaps the greatest outpouring of loyalty to the crown in Central Alberta's history.

While most of the news dealt with the thrill of the Royal Visit, there were also increasing numbers of reports about an impending war in Europe. Ironically, although the 1920s and 1930s had generally been times of economic troubles for Red Deer and area, they had also been times of peace. Now that the hard times were ending, the era of peace was drawing to a close as well.

On September 3, 1939, the expected and feared event finally happened. Great Britain declared war on Germany after the German invasion of Poland. One week later Canada joined the hostilities. For the second time in twenty-five years, a terrible global conflict had broken out, and another era of Red Deer's history had abruptly ended.

Chapter 7

The Second War

LEFT: Airmen from #36 SFTS (Penhold Airbase) joined this march to help boost the Victory Loan campaign in May 1943.

ABOVE: Recruitment poster from the Second World War. Enlistment rates in the Red Deer area were among the highest in Canada.

For the second time in a generation, the scourge of world war had descended upon Central Alberta and the rest of the nation. However, in contrast to the situation in 1914, Canada did not automatically enter the great conflict when Great Britain made its declaration of war. Instead the Canadian Parliament waited for several days before voting for a declaration of hostilities against Germany and its allies.

The delay was largely motivated by the Canadian government's desire to demonstrate its political independence from Great Britain. It was also prompted by a reluctance to become immediately immersed in another total war. The memories of the terrible casualties, economic disruptions and the social upheavals of the First Great War were still strong. The Canadian government realized the necessity of meeting the Nazi challenge to freedom and democracy, but it also wanted to temper the enormous costs of such a struggle.

This is not to suggest that the federal authorities did nothing to prepare for the outbreak of war. For many months both the

The members of the
78th Field Battery, Royal
Canadian Artillery in
the summer of 1939.

permanent force and militia units had been strengthened. During the summer of 1939 several thousands of dollars worth of improvements were made to the Penhold airport, including the relocation of the radio beacon from the south side of Red Deer.

On September 1, 1939, the military authorities ordered the complete mobilization of the Canadian Army Active Force. Over the next three days, thirteen militia men from the 78th Field Battery left Red Deer for Esquimalt, British Columbia, where they joined the coastal defence artillery.

A decision was made not to bring the 78th Battery up to full war strength. Instead, recruitment commenced at the armoury for an Edmonton unit, the 92nd Battery. As had been the case at the start of the First World War, the local men quickly responded to the new call to arms. On September 11, the day after the formal declaration of war, thirty men left Red Deer to train with the 92nd Battery, and a week later another twenty-four followed them to

Edmonton. A number of men also left to enlist in such Calgary units as the 23rd Battery and the Calgary Highlanders. As the military got its mobilization program under way, work on organizing the home front began. On September 21, 1939, more than 130 people turned out to reorganize the moribund Red Deer branch of the Canadian Red Cross Society. A fund-raising drive was initiated, and a sum of more than $1500 was quickly raised.

By mid-October the pace of recruitment began to slacken. Most of the units which were to make up the First Canadian Division had met their quotas, and the military authorities had no immediate plans to mobilize new units. In a speech made in Red Deer, Brigadier George Pearkes explained that the intention was to train the troops in Canada thoroughly before sending them overseas. He added that the authorities felt it was more efficient to handle the recruits in batches rather than in a continual stream.

The lack of urgency was reinforced by

the unusual quiet along the fronts. There were a few skirmishes, air raids and submarine attacks. However, most military leaders expected the same style of trench warfare that had existed in the First World War. They consequently directed most of their attention to preparing defences and building the strengths of their fighting forces rather than to launching offensives.

By early 1940 there was growing criticism of the federal government's conduct of the war. As a result Prime Minister Mackenzie King called a federal election to secure a new mandate. Premier Aberhart cunningly called a provincial election for the same time. The Liberals and Conservatives of the Unity movement now found themselves in the awkward position of campaigning against Social Credit in the provincial contest and against each other in the federal election.

Across the province Premier Aberhart's strategy worked well, and the Social Credit government was returned, albeit with a much reduced majority. In Red Deer, however, the anti-Social Credit feelings remained strong, and Alfred Speakman, the former UFA Member of Parliament, was elected by a comfortable margin. In the federal election five days later, the Social Credit candidate F.D. Shaw won the riding, but

in the City of Red Deer he finished third behind the Liberals and Conservatives.

Ironically, two weeks after Primer Minister Mackenzie King received the electoral endorsement of his policies of caution and restraint, the war changed dramatically. The German launched their stunning Blitzkrieg offensive. In a few brief weeks they seized Denmark and Norway and then swept across Belgium, Holland and France. The great defences of the Western Front collapsed. By the late spring of 1940, Great Britain and its Commonwealth allies were left to fight on alone against the victorious German forces.

Almost immediately, new enlistment drives were commenced across Canada. The 78th Battery was ordered to mobilize at once as part of a new active-service unit with the 22nd Battery from Gleichen, Alberta. In two days more than forty recruits reported at the armoury. Within two weeks, 150 men had enlisted in the artillery.

Shortly thereafter, the military authorities announced that a company of the Calgary Regiment (Tank) would be raised in Red Deer. In one day, more than seventy men volunteered to join the unit, and the company quickly met its quota of 150 men.

Manpower was not only needed for mil-

Men of the Non-Permanent Active Militia Training Centre (NPAMTC) #130 photographed in front of Central School in the fall of 1940.

The front gate of the new militia training centre constructed north of Fifth Street North (55th Street) by the federal government in 1940. The cost of servicing the new camp forced the City of Red Deer to borrow money from the bank for the first time since 1924.

itary service. Crews were hired to start work on an expansion of the Penhold airport. Earlier in the year the airfield had been chosen as a training base under the British Commonwealth Air Training Plan, a joint program of Canada, Great Britain, Australia and New Zealand. With the crisis in Europe deepening each day, plans were accelerated and the construction work was pushed forward at a frenetic pace.

Despite these various initiatives there was a widespread feeling that not enough was being done for the war. The Red Deer Board of Trade held a special meeting in June 1940 and passed five resolutions demanding more speed and vigour in the war effort, the internment of all subversives, registration of foreigners, conscription of manpower and wealth, and more stringent regulations on the sale of firearms and explosives. Plans were also made to hold a massive public meeting which would demand more action from the government.

While the Board of Trade was voicing its concerns and opinions, the federal government passed the National Resources Mobilization Act, which authorized compulsory selective service for home defence and civil employment. With the adoption of these new measures, the Board of Trade's mass meeting was changed into a "Stop Hitler"

rally which sought to marshal public support for the war effort rather than to express grievances against the government.

The rally was an outstanding success and reflected the enormous readiness of the townspeople to "do their bit" for the war effort. A special appeal for funds to buy an ambulance for the Red Cross had a strong response with contributions growing to nearly $2,000 very quickly. Service clubs such as the Kinsmen undertook to promote the sale of war-savings certificates, while the Rotary Club decided to raise funds for refugee relief.

One special community endeavour began in early July 1940, when Red Deer welcomed the first of its "war guests." These were usually young children, sometimes accompanied by their mothers, who were being evacuated from England as the great Battle of Britain was about to erupt. On one occasion a ship carrying some children bound for Central Alberta was torpedoed by a German submarine, but fortunately all of the young passengers were rescued.

As the summer progressed, the 78th Battery was reorganized as a unit of the Non-permanent Active Militia, and another round of recruitment began. A decision was also made to form a Red Deer battalion of the Alberta Veterans' Volunteer Reserve.

Within a brief period of time, a number of First World War veterans joined this home guard unit.

On August 7, 1940, the federal government announced the construction of a militia training centre in Red Deer. For the 2,500 residents of the city, the scope of the facility was staggering. More than thirty buildings were to be constructed on a twenty-hectare site northeast of fifth Street North (55th Street) and Waskasoo (45th) Avenue. Thirty-two officers and another 150 non-commissioned officers and men were to be stationed at the camp. As well, up to 1,000 men were to be accommodated during a four-week training period.

Work on the camp began almost immediately. Soon nearly 200 tradesmen were employed on the site. With an even larger number of men working on the Penhold airport, and with several others employed on civilian projects such as the new wing of the Municipal Hospital and the new public Intermediate School for Grades Seven, Eight and Nine, a critical shortage of labour developed.

Moreover, the new militia centre meant that the city had to provide extensive sewer, water and electrical power hookups. With the cost of these utility installations exceeding $15,000, the city was forced to borrow money from the bank to meet current expenses for the first time since 1924.

Throughout the fall the community hastily prepared for the imminent onslaught of soldiers to the city. A coordinating committee of fifteen organizations was formed to arrange for the soldiers' entertainments. The Citizens' Band was resurrected after being dormant for over two years. The public school board, after some debate, agreed to let the soldiers use the gymnasium in the Intermediate School on one night a week. A member of the Board of Trade suggested that with the large number of newcomers arriving in the city shortly, perhaps the time had come to have all the streets and avenues clearly marked and the houses numbered. The aldermen decided, however, that with all the extraordinary expenses they were currently facing, this would be one extra project that they could not afford.

Despite all the activity surrounding the new militia training centre, the community continued to busy itself with such home-front efforts as the National War Loan campaign. The city and military officials decided that with all of the news reports of the bombing raids on England, Red Deer would be "bombed" with leaflets promoting the bond drive. Unfortunately, the scheme was not a great success. Most of the pamphlets

Despite the outbreak of the Second World War, the Red Deer Public School Board was able to construct a much-needed Intermediate School for grades seven, eight and nine in 1940.

Men of the 69th Tank Transporter Company, Royal Canadian Army Service Corps (RCASC) were among the hundreds who trained at the A–20 Camp in Red Deer during the war.

were blown well north of the city by the wind and only a few fell on their intended targets.

In early October 1940 the militia training centre was finally ready to be opened. However, as often happens with well-planned and rehearsed events, there was chaos when 200 men showed up one day earlier than expected. The military authorities spent a frantic evening trying to find bunks for all of the men and enough rations to feed them supper. Eventually, all of the snags were straightened out. The next day the first group of 900 men received their medical examinations and began their one-month period of training.

As the militia camp became fully operational, its impact was felt throughout the city and the Village of North Red Deer. Restaurants found it necessary to expand their premises, and the local hotels enlarged their beer parlours. A number of the officers and permanent staff at the camp decided to bring their families to Red Deer to live. As a result, although several new residences were built, there was a growing shortage of housing. As well, school enrolment rose sharply and the public school board again found itself with full classrooms despite the opening of the new Intermediate School.

In the second week of November, the

first class of soldiers at the militia centre finished their prescribed period of training with an air raid. A few days later the next group of 1,000 trainees started their stint at the camp. Their arrival in Red Deer coincided with the sudden appearance of winter. Several centimetres of snow fell and temperatures plunged to -30° C. While the cold weather allowed the city's staff to flood three open-air skating rinks, it also made life miserable for many of the soldiers. A round of influenza swept through the camp, and several dozen men were laid up in the camp hospital, which did not have all of its furnaces hooked up.

Disease was not the only unsettling occurrence at the camp. In December 1940 four men were charged under the Criminal Code with pilfering $5 worth of "regimental necessities" from the camp kitchen. Their haul included two kilograms of halibut, a five kilogram pail of drippings and a hard old piece of cheese. The defence lawyer argued that the food was unfit for human consumption, but the prosecutor contended that the cheese at least could have been used with macaroni. The men were convicted and given heavy fines.

In another case a young soldier on leave got too boisterous on a local bus and was ordered to take another. He took the sug-

gestion literally and was caught driving the borrowed vehicle near Ponoka. He too was convicted, given a $100 fine and deprived of the rest of his leave.

Early in 1941 the third group of trainees arrived at the militia training camp. A new round of recruiting was conducted for the 2–78th Field Battery at the Armoury. In February the Calgary Regiment (Tank) was mobilized and became the 14th Army Tank Battalion (Calgary Regiment). Nearly 130 local men enlisted in the unit. In March a huge crowd saw them off in Calgary when they left for further training at Camp Borden in Ontario.

Meanwhile, the federal government announced that the training period for men called up under the National Service Act would be extended to four months from thirty days. Consequently, in March 1941 the military authorities announced that the militia training centre would be changed into an eight-week advanced training camp for the Royal Canadian Army Service

Corps. The new centre, which was named A–20, was to include 100 officers, 550 instructors, 500 active service men and 500 recruits in training. Work began on a number of new buildings and large quantities of equipment and vehicles were transferred to Red Deer from other military installations.

While the new construction work got under way at the A–20 camp, the work at the Penhold airport had progressed to the point that the military authorities were able to turn the base temporarily into No. 2A Manning Depot for the Royal Canadian Air Force (RCAF). As such, the facility was used for the initial training of fresh recruits prior to their being assigned to flying, wireless or other training centres.

As the number of men and women in active service continued to mount, a decision was made by the federal authorities to have one coordinated national charity drive to raise funds for personal comforts and services. In March 1941 a joint appeal on behalf of the Salvation Army, YMCA,

On November 16, 1940, the first Royal Canadian Air Force (RCAF) personnel arrived at Penhold. Later, the base was taken over by the Royal Air Force (RAF).

In June 1941 the Royal Canadian Navy launched a new Bangor-class minesweeper named the *HMCS Red Deer*.

of the war. In contrast to the situation of only a few years before, jobs were now plentiful, wages were rising, business profits were increasing and local farmers were enjoying both abundant harvests and good prices for their produce. Instead of economic hardship and suffering, the war had engendered the best boom for Red Deer in thirty years.

The signs of the boom were everywhere. The CADP, which had been losing a great deal of money in the late 1930s, was now making a sizeable profit and consequently built a large addition onto its milk condensery. A new creamery was constructed on Ross Street by United Dairies, while Red Deer Bottling began building a new soft-drink works on Gaetz Avenue South. A cold storage locker plant was established near the CPR station, and throughout the city several new houses were built.

The wartime economy had some serious detriments. By the summer of 1941 there were growing shortages of several essential products. Sales of gasoline were cut off in Red Deer in the evenings and on Sundays. Inflation began to reappear. However, unlike the situation during the First World War, the federal government took strong corrective measures. In October 1941 the powers of the Wartime Prices and Trade Board were enormously expanded. Stringent wage and price controls were imposed and plans were set to implement a system of rationing.

The war also brought personal grief and suffering. In August 1940 the first man in Red Deer to have enlisted, Ben Long, became the first to be lost when he was killed in an accident in Manitoba. Three other men died of illness while on active service. In July 1941 a pilot in the RCAF, Matt Dunham, became the first local resident to be killed in action. The tragedy of war was starting to strike home.

During the summer of 1941 Red Deer was honoured by the Royal Canadian Navy when a new Bangor-class minesweeper was

Knights of Columbus, Royal Canadian Legion and IODE was launched with a nation-wide objective of $5.5 million. Organizers in Red Deer and area expected to raise between $3,000 and $3,500, but to their surprise more than $8,000 in contributions and pledges were received.

Immediately after the end of this War Services Drive, the federal government began its Victory Loan Campaign to sell bonds to finance the war effort. The Red Deer and District quota was set at $177,000. In order to get the appeal off to a strong and emotional start, the local officials organized the largest parade of military personnel and equipment in Red Deer's history. More than 3,000 people turned out for the event. Within a month the local organizers proudly reported that 132 percent of the quota had been raised.

The great successes of the Victory Loan, War Services and other fund-raising campaigns reflected the tremendous increase in prosperity in the community since the start named after the city. While only one Central Albertan ever served on the ship, a sense of camaraderie developed between the townspeople and the sailors. Letters and gifts were continually exchanged and the local newspaper carefully followed the ship's activities and adventures.

In August 1941 construction work on the Penhold airport was finally completed. The RCAF discontinued the use of the facility as a manning depot and turned it over to the RAF for its new use as a service flying training school. On August 20, 1941, the first contingent of 600 airmen arrived at the base. Unfortunately, actual flight training was slow in getting started. There was a critical shortage of qualified instructors and initially only twenty planes were on hand.

Despite these handicaps, the pressures of the war made it imperative to use all resources to the utmost and to continue the recruitment and training of personnel. The military authorities began construction of another flying training school south of the Penhold air base near the Village of Bowden. Meanwhile, the Canadian Woman's Army Corps recruited and stationed three companies in Red Deer for clerical, motor transport and commissariat duties.

With the hundreds of airmen at Penhold and the hundreds of soldiers and other personnel at the A—20 camp, many people felt that there should be a public recreation centre in the city. There was great consternation in the community when the Auxiliary War Services Board in Ottawa vetoed a proposal to build a new hall despite the offer of city council to pay one-half of the costs. After the public protests went unheeded, the aldermen decided to proceed on their own initiative. An old furniture store on First Street South (49th Street) was purchased and $3,000 were spent on the necessary renovations. City council then leased the building for $70 per month to the Knights of Columbus, who had agreed to act as the facility's operators. Despite the

PRICE 5 CENTS

THE PENHOLD LOG

CANADA   ALBERTA

36 S · F · T · S

RAF

DECEMBER
VOLUME I

1941
NUMBER 1

In 1941 the #36 Service Flying Training School (SFTS) opened under the command of the RAF.

rather ad hoc nature of the project, it proved to be a great success. Within a short period of time the management reported as many as 1,000 visitors a day and an average of 3,700 a week.

The success of the Knights of Columbus Hut and the return of unseasonably mild weather to Central Alberta may have brought some joy to the community, but such feelings were more than offset by the grim news from overseas. In December 1941 Hong Kong was captured by the Japanese and Horace Gerard became the first local man to be taken prisoner of war. Shortly thereafter, word was received that three local young men serving with the air force had been killed and another serving in the navy had been lost at sea. In a small city where

ABOVE: In 1942 city council purchased an old furniture store and leased it to the Knights of Columbus as an entertainment and refreshment centre for soldiers and airmen.

BELOW: Plane crashes, such as this one south of Red Deer, became all too common during the Second World War. In four years, thirty-five young airmen from Penhold were killed while in training.

people generally knew one another, the sense of loss and anguish was widespread.

There were also tragedies close to home. In late December 1941 LAC D.A. Phillips died from injuries sustained in a plane crash. He was the first of thirty-five young airmen stationed at Penhold to be killed in flying accidents in Central Alberta. Military funerals were to become almost a monthly occurrence in the city.

Early in 1941 members of the various war auxiliaries met to form the Red Deer Home Comforts Fund. There was a concern in the community that some who were serving their country were being missed or neglected. There was also a desire to ensure that the provision of comforts and services was handled as expeditiously and efficiently as possible. Work began immediately on a comprehensive list of those on active service. A

number of fund-raising projects were organized, including Saturday night dances at the Armoury.

In February 1941 the federal government commenced its Second Victory Loan canvass and set Red Deer's quota at $137,000. The bond drive was to be kicked off with a Beacon Fire of Freedom on Ross Street by the City Hall, but cold weather forced the cancellation of the ceremonial bonfire. Ironically, a few hours before the event was to take place, a blaze caused several thousand dollars worth of damage to a downtown business block. Nevertheless, the loan campaign proceeded smoothly, and within a brief period of time, the Red Deer organizers had reached 128 percent of their goal.

The Victory Loan drive received a big boost when city council decided to buy several thousand dollars worth of bonds with surplus city funds. After the brief disruption caused by the construction of the militia training centre in 1940, the municipal coffers had begun to swell again, despite further cuts in property and business tax rates.

Not all of the city's extra funds were invested in the government's war bonds. An extension was built on City Hall and Gaetz Avenue was paved. After much cajoling from the chief of police, city council finally agreed to buy a second-hand police car. The aldermen also reversed their decision on house numbering and agreed to spend several hundred dollars on buying metal letters for all of the houses and business blocks in the city.

The letters purchased were made of zinc because supplies of other metals such as aluminum, iron and steel were scarce. The problem had become so acute that a proposal by Northwestern Utilities to provide the city with natural gas service had to be scrubbed because the company was unable to secure a sufficient quantity of steel pipe.

In order to help alleviate these shortages of metal, a national "Scrap Hitler With

Scrap" campaign was organized. The Red Deer Salvage Committee was able to collect several tons of cast iron and steel. City council even contributed to the cause the First World War field guns which had been displayed on the City Square since 1919. The demands of the war were so great, however, that these tremendous efforts made little impact on the problem.

There were also serious and growing shortages of a number of other goods and materials. In the late spring of 1942, ration cards were distributed for such items as sugar, and special permits had to be obtained to purchase rubber tires. A few months later the government announced that ration books for sugar, tea, coffee and other staples would soon be issued.

As the demands and restrictions on the civilian population grew, there was an increasingly strident call on the federal government to institute conscription for overseas military service. Because of the divisiveness of the 1917 conscription crisis, the Prime Minister wanted to avoid such a measure. Finally, he was forced to relent, and he called a national plebiscite on the question for April 27, 1942. Red Deer voted yes to the new conscription plan by a tally of 1,300 to 141, while most of the rest of the country agreed by almost as strong of a margin.

Ironically, the demand for overseas conscription came at a time when the Canadian Army had seen little actual fighting. Canadian airmen and sailors had been embroiled in the Battle of Britain and the Battle of the Atlantic, but most of the Canadian soldiers were still in training in either Great Britain or Canada.

The situation changed on August 19, 1942, when 5,000 men, including those in the Calgary Tank Regiment, landed on the coast of France in a raid on the port of Dieppe. The losses were horrendous. More than 900 men were killed and nearly 2,000 were taken prisoner of war. For nearly a month the townspeople of Red Deer were

left wondering about the fate of several local men. Eventually, the word came that twenty-one were being held as POWs.

While the community was still anxiously awaiting the awful news about the losses at Dieppe, the townspeople were thrown into a tumult by an incident on the south side of the city. A crew of a freight train very nearly ran over a soldier from the A–20 camp who was lying bound and gagged on the tracks. The badly shaken fellow told the trainmen that he had been kidnapped by two German-speaking strangers who demanded that he provide them with information on local munitions supplies and troop movements. He claimed that when he had been unable to answer their questions, he had been left on the tracks to die.

After two days of interrogation and no sign of the alleged assailants, the police

ABOVE: Two fund-raising booths at the annual Red Deer Fair in 1943. Home Front organizations – such as the 13th Field Regiment Women's Auxiliary, the 92nd Battery Ladies Auxiliary and the Home Comforts Fund – played an invaluable role throughout the war in sending packages and letters to those serving overseas.

BELOW: Prisoners of war at Stalag VIIIB. Included in the photograph are several Red Deer and area men, including Ken Smethurst, Fred Hilsabeck, Dennis Scott, Stan Playdon, Gus Nelson, Owen Richards, Jim Hilsabeck, Cliff Hooey and Charles Reinhart.

Damage east of Gaetz Avenue caused by a sudden thaw in early April 1943. The flood was one of the worst ever along the Red Deer River.

began to suspect the soldier's story. They finally concluded that he had tied himself up and had gone into shock when he was unable to release himself before the train reached him. The soldier was charged with attempted suicide, and the local citizens were relieved to learn that "enemy agents" were not lurking about the city.

In mid-October 1942 the local authorities decided to stage some dramatics of their own to publicize the launch of the Third Victory Loan. They organized a blackout and mock air raid, and a week later simulated an occupation of the city by "enemy" soldiers. The theatrics went well and once again, the residents of Red Deer contributed far more than had been expected.

On November 15 and 16, 1942, the worst storm since late December 1924, struck

Airmen from the RAF make a Christmas shopping trip to Osborne's Ladies Wear in Red Deer to buy lingerie for loved ones back home, 1943.

Best wishes for Christmas and the New Year from Oflag VII B. 1943.

Central Alberta. Although the temperatures did not initially drop too severely, there was a very heavy snowfall which made the city's streets impassable. However, the severity of the storm presaged the brutal conditions of the coming winter.

The harshness of the weather was compounded by an acute shortage of coal throughout the district. By January 1943 fuel had become so scarce that the public school board was forced to shut down the schools periodically. Many public meetings were moved from the large halls and auditoriums into smaller, warmer rooms. Even city council decided to move its meetings from the council chamber into the cozier city office.

The military did its best to help out in the crisis. Convoys of soldiers were dispatched to mine emergency supplies of coal. It was not an easy task. Temperatures

This Canadian Army Band included several Red Deer and area men. Pictured are Sid Bearchell, Bernie Karsh, Frank Kosler, Fraser Greenback, Frank Bailley, Tommy Lynass, Fred Beddington, Chuck Yakimchuck, Walter Fisher and Frank Hosak.

Doris Forbes and her pet beaver, Mickey, who became famous throughout Alberta. At the 1943 Red Deer Fair, Mickey proved to be an excellent fund-raising draw for the war effort.

plunged to as low as -45° C. The trucks got stuck in snowdrifts or else slipped into the ditches. All too often the vehicles used up their meagre supplies of gasoline before the soldiers made it back to Red Deer.

Some people managed to keep their sense of humour through the adversity. One popular story held that a local man had been so busy during the cold snap carrying coal in the front door while his wife was carrying the ashes out the back door that they did not see each other until the weather finally warmed up.

While the return of balmier temperatures eased the fuel crisis, shortages of other goods and materials continued. In February 1943 the government issued a second set of ration books with more than 8,000 being distributed in Red Deer and district. The government also imposed stiff reductions in the allowable sales of beer and liquor. The *Red Deer Advocate* reported that some outlets used up their daily quotas in as little as one-half hour, and one journalist expressed

relief that the liquor store was next door to the newspaper office.

Shortages also extended to the city police force, which had trouble finding recruits. Finally, the aldermen decided to phase out the local constabulary and to sign a policing agreement with the RCMP. The Mounties had manpower problems of their own, but their greater supply of resources allowed them to establish a Red Deer detachment on April 1, 1943.

Spring breakup began in early April. Although the end of the hard winter was welcomed by Central Albertans, the quick thaw brought a new set of problems. An ice jam formed on the Red Deer River, and within a few hours the water level rose nearly seven metres. A local feed lot operator lost over 100 animals and several homes were flooded. Ironically, there was a shortage of domestic water in the city as the water treatment plant was washed out of commission. The army agreed to try to dynamite the jam, but before they finished their preparations, the ice gave way on its own. It was a spectacular end to one of the worst floods in Red Deer's history.

As the weather continued to improve and the land began to dry up, the local farmers resumed the threshing which had come to an abrupt halt with the heavy snows of the previous fall. Unfortunately, the wet conditions and an epidemic of mice had a very detrimental effect on the quality of the harvest.

If the local farmers had suffered a setback, it did not seem to affect the Fourth Victory Loan campaign, which was launched on May 1, 1943, with a mass military parade. Twelve days later there was a spectacular fireworks display to celebrate the fact that Red Deer had raised $83,000 more than the $340,000 objective which had been set by the campaign organizers.

The immense success of the latest war-bond drive did not seem to impair the local Elks Club's efforts to raise funds for a wading pool on the City Square. By late June construction work had started. Seven weeks later a large number of children turned out for the official opening ceremonies.

In the early summer of 1943 the long wait of the Canadian Army for combat duty came to an end when the First Infantry Division joined in the successful invasion of Sicily. Among the troops deployed were several Red Deer and area men who had enlisted in artillery units such as the 92nd Battery.

During the first week of August, the annual Red Deer Fair was held. The 92nd Women's Auxiliary received a big boost in their fund-raising efforts when the Wallace Forbes family lent their pet beaver, Mickey, as a special attraction. Mickey had been found as an orphan kit in 1939 and had quickly become so famous that several thousand people were eager to pay a small fee to see him.

During the fall of 1943, the city began to take measures to avoid a repeat of the previous winter's fuel crisis. More than 100 cords of firewood and 150 tons of coal were purchased as emergency supplies. The community also began to plan for the eventual end of the war. In November the Central Alberta Post-War Reconstruction and Rehabilitation Committee was formed. There was a proposal to build a special housing development for veterans. The idea of constructing a memorial community hall was also discussed and debated.

While people were looking forward to a future of peace, there were continual reminders that the war was far from over. The RCAF was conducting mass nighttime bombing raids over Germany, and the Canadian Army was embroiled in the invasion of Italy. The *Red Deer Advocate* reported that six more local residents had lost their lives in the service of their country and a number of others had been wounded. On the home front, two days of the week, Tuesdays and Fridays, were designated as meat-

Their Faith in You is Boundless Keep it so!

Buy the NEW

VICTORY BONDS

SPACE DONATED BY
THE BREWING INDUSTRY OF ALBERTA

Posters were used throughout the war to promote even more sales of Victory Bonds to support the war effort.

less days and the newspaper had to suspend all new subscriptions because of a scarcity of newsprint.

As the year drew to a close, politics again became a burning issue in the community. Red Deer's Independent MLA, Alfred Speakman, passed away suddenly and a by-election was called for December 16, 1943. In contrast to the bitter contest of 1940, Social Credit had become somewhat more popular as fewer and fewer people viewed it as a radical and dangerous movement. Moreover, Premier Aberhart had passed away earlier in the year and had been replaced by the young Ernest Manning. The by-election results confirmed that the partisan tides had turned. The Social Credit candidate, David Ure, was elected by a margin of 185 votes.

There was also a major change in the realm of municipal government. On December 31, 1943, the five rural municipalities in Central Alberta were amalgamated into a new larger district known as the Municipal District of Penhold. Early in 1944 the new councillors decided that the Municipal District of Red Deer was a more appropriate name and voted to locate their administrative offices in the city. A problem of finding affordable office space was solved when Red Deer city council agreed to turn a corner of the building into a public women's washroom and to pay the MD's council $40 a month rent for the convenience.

In the early spring of 1944, the community was caught up in the excitement of some of the best hockey in the history of Central Alberta. Red Deer's A–20 Wheelers included two former members of the NHL and a number of others from national championship teams. The opposing clubs in the Central Alberta Garrison Hockey League were of an equal calibre. The playoff games in March 1944 were closely contested and superbly played matches. Unfortunately, the Wheelers lost their last game to the Calgary Currie team by a score of only 2–1. The men were still local heroes and the Red Deer Board of Trade subsequently held a lavish banquet to honour them.

In the late spring the federal government decided that the need for the British Commonwealth Air Training Plan had diminished and announced that twenty-eight flying training schools, including the one at Penhold, would be closed by December 1944. However, for the residents of Central Alberta, it did not seem that the toll of war was any less. Six young airmen, a soldier and seaman from the district were killed in action. As well, eight RAF trainees from Penhold lost their lives in crashes during the first five months of the year.

The financial costs of the war also remained high, and in May 1944 the Sixth Victory Loan appeal commenced. As had been the case with the previous bond drive in November 1943 and the four earlier efforts, Red Deer's contributions greatly surpassed expectations, and a record $365,000 was raised.

On June 6, 1944, a date now remembered as D-Day, the Allied Forces launched the long-awaited assault on the coast of Normandy in France and opened up the second front against the Germans. Over the next several weeks the Canadian, American and British forces were generally victorious, but at a terrible cost. Seven young men from Red Deer and area lost their lives, and the Canadian forces as a whole suffered more than 18,000 casualties.

The new successes in France and the continuing victories in Italy gave hope to Central Albertans that the war would soon be over. The annual Red Deer Fair in August 1944 was dubbed the Victory Year Fair. In September a committee was formed to make the necessary arrangements for armistice day celebrations.

The hopes for peace proved to be premature. In December 1944 the German Army launched a major counteroffensive. While the attack was eventually stemmed, it slowed the Allied advance and demonstrated that Germany was not about to surrender.

As yet another wartime Christmas approached, the volunteers with the war auxiliaries, the Home Comforts Fund and the Red Cross pressed on with their work of sending Christmas parcels to the troops overseas and to those in the prisoner of war camps. The official farewells were held for the departing Royal Air Force men from Penhold. The personnel at the A–20 camp held an elaborate Christmas party for 200 children with the highlight being the arrival of Santa Claus in a jeep laden with gifts.

Tragically, in the days leading up to Christmas, word was received that five more local lives had been lost overseas. The local

The start of the V-E Day victory parade on Ross Street on May 8, 1945. Leading the marchers are Corporal Mac Hay, Constable Arthur Rosengren and Sergeant Robert Matthewson of the RCMP.

newspaper reported that while the usual holiday parties and gatherings were still held, there was a decidedly sombre note to the normally festive events.

Unfortunately, the first few weeks of the New Year brought little relief from the heartbreaking news. Nine men were killed in battle, three lost their lives in plane crashes and another was taken prisoner. Some people recalled the old saying that the outlook is often the blackest just before the dawn.

In late February came a reminder that the war was indeed coming to an end. The military authorities announced that the A–20 camp would soon be closed and that the facility would be turned into a rehabilitation centre for returned servicemen under the Vocational Training Program. As the operations at the camp wound down, and the RCASC personnel departed, the need for the Knights of Columbus Hut quickly diminished. It too was soon closed, and the building was sold to the Red Deer Elks Club for $7,700.

Throughout the spring of 1945, increasing numbers of veterans returned to their families and friends in Central Alberta. As well, there was the welcome news that some of the POWs had been released. The federal government launched yet another Victory bond drive and cajoled the people to help provide the means to finish the war.

By early May 1945 people realized that the fighting in Europe would be ending very shortly. Plans were renewed for the Victory Day celebrations. Early on Monday, May 7, the news finally arrived. Germany had surrendered.

Schoolchildren arrived for class only to be dismissed for a three-day holiday. Some businesses opened for a brief time, but many remained closed. The authorities also had the government liquor store and the beer parlours shut down for two days.

Everywhere there was great jubilation. Many people gathered on the streets and large numbers flocked to their churches for services of thanksgiving. On May 8 the

The float entered by the Canadian Vocational Training Centre won first prize in the annual Red Deer Parade for its demonstration of machine shop work.

official V-E Day, the civic celebrations were held. A large parade proceeded down Ross Street to the City Square, where despite a bitterly cold wind, a crowd of more than 1,000 had gathered to hear the speeches of the local dignitaries.

Although the hostilities in Europe had ceased, the fight against Japan continued. A number of soldiers and airmen returned to Red Deer on thirty-day leaves pending reassignments to new stations on the Pacific front. However, demobilization work also continued. The CWAC canvassed for more recruits to help with the enormous load of paperwork. The old A–20 camp officially became the Canadian Vocational Training Centre No. 8 on May 14, 1945, and preparations were made to start on trades instruction for recently discharged men. In July the federal government began building twenty-five houses on one-half hectare lots for the returned servicemen.

On August 8, 1945, the *Red Deer Advocate* reported that on the preceding Sunday, a new awesome weapon had been used on the Japanese city of Hiroshima. While the nature of this new atomic bomb was not yet clearly understood, the editor of the paper predicted that "a new epoch in both war and peace is at hand."

On August 14, 1945, word was received

that Japan had surrendered. Across the city the municipal siren, the CPR train whistles and countless automobile horns broke out in a din of celebration. People gathered in the downtown area, and the city officials quickly organized a special street dance on Gaetz Avenue. On the evening of August 15, the official V-J Day, a service of thanksgiving was held on the City Square. Afterward, another outdoor public dance was held. For those who were more sedentary, the Capital Theatre showed the movie *Brother Rat*, which starred an actor named Ronald Reagan and his wife, Jane Wyman.

For the rest of the summer and into the fall, the transition from wartime to peacetime continued. Special gatherings were held to welcome and honour the returning veterans. New fund-raising and clothing drives were held to provide emergency relief supplies to the war-torn regions of Europe. In mid-October the Ninth Victory Loan campaign got under way, and a record $770,000 was raised.

The military authorities began holding huge auction sales to dispose of the massive quantities of surplus materials. After the closure of the RCAF's No. 2 Technical Signals Unit, which had been repairing and rebuilding radio instruments at Penhold, there were widespread reports of the destruction of hundreds of thousands of dollars worth of equipment. The air force replied that only material which was "no longer valuable" was being destroyed.

Meanwhile, the proposal to install natural gas service was revived. On September 24, 1945, the local ratepayers overwhelmingly approved a new bylaw granting the franchise to Northwestern Utilities. A proposal by the councillors of North Red Deer that the village be amalgamated with the city did not meet with as easy a response. There was general agreement on the desirability of such a move, but there were serious reservations about the costs of installing utility services north of the river

Ross Street, looking west toward the Cenotaph, 1945.

and about who would be responsible for paying for them.

There was also a tremendous concern throughout the community about the worsening housing situation. Accommodations had been scarce throughout most of the war, but with the return of the servicemen and the arrival of a number of newcomers, the situation was becoming desperate. Twenty suites were created in the old barracks huts at the CVT Centre, but this was a stopgap measure which only slightly alleviated the crisis.

The housing situation reflected the paradox of the war for Red Deer. Prosperity and progress had returned to the community, and there had been the first significant increase in population in more than thirty years. Although the city's residents had dreamed of such development for a very long time, the wartime shortages and restrictions had hampered the ability of the community to absorb the growth. Hardships had come with the long-sought boom.

The benefits of the wartime economy had also been accompanied by considerable dislocation and grief. More than 1,000 men and women from Red Deer and district had disrupted their lives to go and serve their country. Tragically, fifty-two of them had lost their lives and many more had been wounded. The human costs of the war had been heavy.

In retrospect, the Second World War was a major turning point in Red Deer's history. While the First Great War had been the benchmark between the pioneer boom years and the troubles of the interwar era, the Second World War marked the transition from a small, quiet parkland community to a burgeoning modern centre. Old Red Deer was fading into the past and a new city was taking its place.

Chapter 8

A Beacon to the Future

LEFT: Ross Street, looking east, 1950. The postwar period was a time of tremendous growth, prosperity and change for the City of Red Deer.

ABOVE: During the 1950s there was a veritable explosion of oil exploration activity in the Red Deer area.

As Central Alberta entered the postwar era, Red Deer experienced an incredible tide of change. Although there was a plethora of vexing problems and troublesome disruptions to the old patterns of community life, the general trend was toward phenomenal growth and progress. Because of the many years of either war or economic adversity, people did not react with the same wild enthusiasm that had existed during the pioneer boom times. Nevertheless, there was a growing realization that times had taken a turn for the better and a bright future finally lay ahead.

Many historians view February 13, 1947, as the start of the wonderful new era of prosperity. That was the date when the Imperial Oil Company made its famous discovery of oil near the Town of Leduc. Extensive drilling programs by Imperial and numerous other companies quickly followed, but it was the spectacular fire in the spring of 1948 at the Atlantic No. 3 well that served as the beacon which brought world-wide attention to the momentous new discoveries.

LEFT: In the late 1940s the streets of Red Deer were torn up to allow the installation of the new natural gas mains. This photograph shows work north from the intersection of 40th Avenue and 52nd Street.

RIGHT: On August 22, 1947, a large crowd watched in the rain as Mayor Harvey "Doc" Halladay lit a symbolic flare to inaugurate the new gas service to the city.

While most of the drilling activity took place north of the Red Deer district, there was still a significant local economic impact because of the city's traditional role as a transportation centre. The rail yards were soon full of oil tanker cars and boxcars laden with drilling supplies. There was also a substantial increase in motorized freight, a development which was reflected in the decision by Canadian Pacific to make Red Deer a regional distribution centre for its new trucking operations.

However, the economic boom had actually begun in Red Deer well before the Leduc discoveries. The prosperity of the war years continued as the developments which had been restrained or delayed by wartime restrictions now surged ahead. There was an astonishing amount of construction activity as the community strove to accommodate five dozen new businesses and a 35 percent increase in population since 1941.

There had been some petroleum exploration work carried out west of Red Deer during 1945 and 1946. As well, an aspect of the new oil and gas era had commenced in Red Deer a mere forty days after the end of the war when the new natural gas franchise agreement was approved. Throughout 1946 large crews of men busily laid the transmission lines from the Viking gas fields to the

northeast, and the following year household and business hookups began. On August 22, 1947, a crowd of several hundred braved a cold and rainy night to watch Mayor H.W. Halladay inaugurate the gas service by lighting a special flare next to the City Hall.

To the community the ceremonial flare was a beacon to the future. More than 800 households and nearly all of the businesses now had a clean, efficient and relatively inexpensive source of heating to replace the traditional wood and coal. The atmosphere over the city quite literally began to clear. A sign was later erected on the brow of the North Hill which boasted "Look Up, The Cleanest Sky In The World Is Above You."

Despite the obvious benefits, the arrival of the natural gas service was accompanied by a number of complaints, criticism and apprehensions. Several residents expressed annoyance when shortages of pipe and meters caused delays in their hookups. Others protested when their well-established lawns and gardens were torn up. Some did not want to have the mains near their homes because they worried about the possibilities of gas explosions.

When Northwestern Utilities successfully asked city council to adopt a simpler system of street numbering, the Old Timers' Association objected to the loss of

historical names. As a result a compromise was struck whereby the new 50th Street and 50th Avenue also kept their old designations as Ross Street and Gaetz Avenue. Ironically, in spite of the controversy, most residents continued to orient themselves by old landmarks, and some time passed before someone noticed that several of the new street signs had the wrong numbers on them.

The crossing of the local streams posed special challenges to the installation of the main gas transmission lines. At the Blindman River, Northwestern Utilities used an unique suspension bridge. In Red Deer arrangements were made with the provincial government to have the mains attached to the new traffic bridge which was being built to replace the 1909 structure.

Construction of the new bridge started in the summer of 1946, but with the incredible amount of other building activity, progress was hampered by shortages of steel and concrete. In mid-March 1947 tragedy struck when an ice jam caused a sudden

flood. Five women and children who were residing in a temporary shack next to the jobsite were drowned. The ice did very little damage to the piers, however, and work on the superstructure resumed later in the spring. By December 1947 the bridge was finally finished. As part of the opening ceremonies, the mayors of North and South Red Deer cut a symbolic log in half with a crosscut saw.

The ceremony was one of the last official acts of the mayor of North Red Deer. During the fall of 1947, the ratepayers of the village overwhelmingly voted in favour of a new proposal to amalgamate with the city, even though it meant that they would have to pay a special ten-mill tax levy to cover the cost of new utility services. On Christmas Eve the village council held its final meeting. On January 1, 1948, the two communities were officially merged.

While the village and city councils were proceeding with their successful amalgamation negotiations, the Red Deer Public

A 1950 aerial shot of North Red Deer taken after its amalgamation with the City of Red Deer. The new traffic bridge can be seen at the top of the photograph. St. Joseph's Convent appears in the foreground.

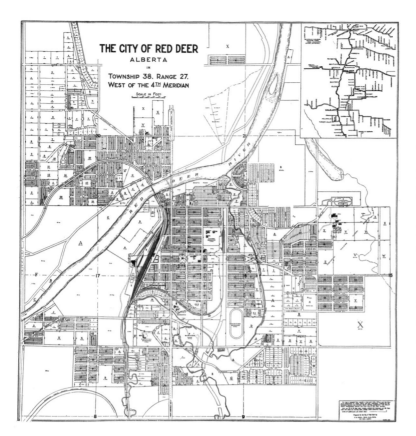

THE CITY OF RED DEER
ALBERTA
IN
TOWNSHIP 38. RANGE 27.
WEST OF THE 4TH MERIDIAN
SCALE IN FEET

A 1947 map shows the newly expanded City of Red Deer following the amalgamation with the Village of North Red Deer.

School District No. 104, which had always included both sides of the river, entered into an unprecedented cooperative relationship with the Rocky Mountain House, Lacombe and Red Deer (rural) school divisions. A new form of secondary education, a composite high school with vocational and academic instruction, was established. Classroom and dormitory accommodations were secured in the buildings at the old A–20 army camp. The public school board was then able to convert the high school building on 48th Avenue into much-needed classroom space for junior grades and dropped plans to build new schoolhouses in North Red Deer and on the south side of the city.

The huts at the old army camp had only been built as temporary wartime structures and their shortcomings caused innumerable problems. Lighting in several of the dormitories was poor, heating was often inadequate and there was an outbreak of cockroaches in the washrooms. As well, the ini-

tial joint administrative arrangement did not work very well, and there was considerable dissension, particularly among the dormitory staff. Consequently, in 1948 the Red Deer School Division, which had greater access than the public district to provincial equalization grants, assumed full responsibility for the school. The other boards then paid tuition fees for the students from their jurisdictions.

In spite of the difficulties the "Comp" proved to be an educational success and attracted students from all over Alberta as well as from other parts of Canada. In 1949 the school became even more of an unique institution when the trimester system was adopted. The flexibility which resulted from dividing the school year into three terms was particularly advantageous to rural students who had to work on the farm in the spring or fall. As a result the nonresident enrolment rose significantly.

As a spirit of cooperation and progress emerged in municipal and educational affairs, there was an increasingly urgent need for a similar initiative in the affairs of the hospital. With the enormous increase in the local population, a large addition to the hospital building had become essential. However, in order to properly finance such a project and become eligible for special provincial and federal grants, the boundaries of the hospital district had to be expanded to include the rural areas surrounding the city.

Although earlier proposals had been defeated in plebiscites, the council of the Municipal District of Red Deer agreed in principle to the enlargement of the hospital district in January 1948. Surprisingly it was not until the spring of 1949 that the ratepayers ratified this decision and agreed to pay one-half of the cost of a new $400,000 extension to the hospital building. Actual construction work was delayed for yet another year. With the existing facility operating at 140 percent of capacity, the hospital board was forced to acquire the old administration building from the A–20 camp for use as a temporary ward and later as a nurses' residence.

While progress at the hospital was slow, a joint effort by the new Red Deer Athletic Association, the public school board and the city to create new recreational facilities became mired in difficulties. A site chosen for a new athletic field on the south side of Ross Street, between 47th and 48th Avenues, proved to be a veritable morass. A brush cutter being used to clear the growth of willows became so badly stuck in the mud that a Churchill tank had to be borrowed from the army to free it.

A new location on the south side of the Central schoolyard was selected, but again marshy ground hampered the work of levelling the field. Several local construction firms, the Canadian Vocational Training Centre, the militia, the MD of Red Deer and numerous volunteers pitched in to help finish the job. Nevertheless, the costs of the project had become much higher than anticipated. Very few of the other plans for the site were therefore ever completed.

There were also tribulations for a proposal to build a cultural and recreational centre as a memorial to those who had given their lives during the Second World War. Initially, this complex was to include a swimming pool, gymnasium, auditorium and library. However, a public fund-raising drive managed to raise only $35,000. As had been the case with a similar proposition after the First Great War, this was not enough to cover the costs of the project.

The plans for the centre were subsequently revamped. The public library board unanimously asked to be excluded from the project. City council agreed to proceed with the construction of the swimming pool using funds from the floating of a debenture. The Memorial Centre committee then considered either the construction of a hall next to the pool building or the acquisition

of a hangar from the old Bowden airport, which could be renovated into a gym and auditorium. These schemes proved to be either too expensive or too impractical.

Unfortunately, rapidly increasing construction costs meant that the city underestimated the expense of the pool. Two attempts to have the ratepayers approve an additional $15,000 debenture to finish the building were unsuccessful. The impasse was finally resolved when the city received a $7,000 grant from the provincial government and the Memorial Centre committee made a contribution from the funds they had raised. Ironically, during the official opening of the pool in August 1949, a boy accidentally fell through a plate glass window and his parents sued the city for $16,000 for the injuries he had sustained.

The swimming pool debenture was the first to have been issued by the city since the purchase of the Western General in 1926. With only one brief exception in 1940 when the A–20 camp was built, the city had man-

ABOVE: An outdoor dance held at the Red Deer Composite High School in 1948. In the background are the old army huts of the A–20 camp, which had been converted into classrooms and dormitories.

BELOW: Children taking part in one of the Learn to Swim classes at Red Deer's new outdoor swimming pool on the south side of 49th Street, 1950.

These six postmen – Wes Wagar, Len Green, Harold Gourlay, Ken Smethurst, Archie McBlane and George Morgan – inaugurated Red Deer's first door-to-door delivery in 1948. The improved postal service soon necessitated the construction of a new post office building.

aged for over two decades to meet its current and capital expenses from the general tax levy and utilities surpluses. Moreover, it had been able to retire all of its long-term indebtedness by 1946.

However, with Red Deer's population rising in a mere five years by more than the total number of residents in the prewar era, the city's expenditures began to soar. There were astounding demands for new roads, sidewalks, sewers, waterworks and electrical services. There were expensive repairs and overdue improvements from years of either economic adversity or wartime restriction. There were also costly new undertakings, such as an extensive street paving program and the purchase of most of the old A–20 campsite for housing development.

For a few years, city council attempted to continue the old "pay-as-you-go" policy by increasing revenues. Between 1945 and 1949 the property tax was raised from twenty-eight to forty-five mills and the special ten-mill tax levy, which had been imposed on North Red Deer, was extended to all new subdivisions. Sales of lots which had been seized for taxes in the earlier times of troubles became a lucrative source of revenue, while both the provincial and federal governments boosted their grants for a number of municipal projects.

Nevertheless, by 1949 the utilities surpluses and the old Victory Bond investments had largely been spent. The aldermen were besieged with complaints about the poor conditions of the roads and the slow pace of utilities installations. City council consequently adopted a four-year capital improvement plan, which would be financed with borrowed funds. The first year's issue of $100,000 in debentures received the required two-thirds vote of approval from the ratepayers. Still the two defeats of the supplementary debenture issue for the swimming pool demonstrated that public acceptance of deficit financing was rather weak.

In 1950 the aldermen raised the tax rate to fifty-five mills and proposed the borrowing of another $125,000 for capital projects. However, the ratepayers, concerned about the escalating costs of municipal services and angered over a plan to spend $20,000 on water meter installations, decisively defeated the debenture bylaws. City council responded with an emergency economy program which included the suspension of all public works projects, the passage of a bylaw restricting water consumption and the imposition of a ban on all new home construction, except where water and sewer lines were already available.

An enormous public outcry followed. The largest ratepayers' meeting in Red Deer's history was held in the Armoury. Speaker after speaker vented their frustrations about the state of the city. The aldermen resisted demands to amend or reduce the public works program and cited a consultant's report which recommended hundreds of thousands of dollars in additional projects. Finally, the meeting unanimously passed a resolution of confidence in the city's administration and the debenture bylaws were later ratified in another public vote.

The controversy over municipal finances had been acrimonious, but it was still a product of economic good times rather than recession. The signs of the continuing boom were everywhere. In 1948 the value of building permits issued broke the $1 million mark, and in the following year the total rose by another 50 percent. An American company announced plans to build a $2 million pulp and paper mill on the old E.B. Eddy property, and there were rumours of an oil refinery being built on the south side of the city. In mid-1949 radio station CKRD began broadcasting as the first local operation since CKLC shut down in 1933.

Even the agricultural sector enjoyed relative prosperity despite the challenges of financing the growing trend toward mechanization. The return of the wet cycle, which caused the floods on the river and mired such projects as the new athletic field, also brought wonderful crop yields. The high quality of the local grain was indicated when S.J. Allsop won the world wheat championship in 1947 and 1948, and D.R. Carlyle won the national barley title in 1949.

The economic prosperity and phenomenal growth in the city eventually prompted the federal government to make long-awaited improvements to the local post office. In 1948 door-to-door mail delivery was instituted after the local Legion published a city directory to prove that there were enough households to warrant such a service. In 1950, after thirty-seven years of promises, construction began on an adequate post office building. However, a request by the Red Deer Board of Trade to have twice-daily mail delivery was curtly rejected.

The provincial government also moved to improve its facilities in the city. Construction of a new provincial building for the Treasury Branch, liquor store, police court and various government departments was started in 1949 on the corner of 51st Street and Gaetz Avenue. As well, work began on an $800,000 expansion of the Provincial Training School for the mentally handicapped.

Not all of the new public projects involved the construction of buildings. In

Red Deer's new City Hall Park was initially a subject of controversy, but it eventually became the city's chief beauty spot and the source of considerable local pride.

1949 city council, by a margin of only one vote, agreed to a proposal by the parks superintendent to beautify the downtown area by developing an ornamental park on the west end of the City Square. Several sports groups, service clubs and individual citizens strongly protested the plan. They felt that the square was better suited for such recreational purposes as a baseball diamond, children's playground and open-air skating rink. Others contended that the $1,800 cost of the project was too extravagant. Fortunately, the aldermen, despite their ambivalence, stuck by their decision and the new park eventually became the focus of considerable civic pride.

Since the city's administrators had never been happy with the decision to locate the Cenotaph in the middle of Ross Street, the design of the City Hall Park included a spot in the centre of the gardens for the memorial statue. As well, with the plans for the new Memorial Centre apparently in limbo, there was a growing public consensus that the Cenotaph should be rededicated to include the memory of those who had lost their lives in the Second World War.

This service of rededication was held on November 13, 1949. A few months later, however, the Red Deer School Division and the Memorial Centre Committee made a

A net royalty trust certificate from the Red Deer Leduc Oil Company was part of one venture by a group of local residents to take advantage of the great oil drilling boom of the early 1950s.

joint proposal to build a public auditorium and gymnasium in one of the old drill halls at the former A–20 army camp. The community responded warmly to the new idea, and the extra funds needed for the project were quickly raised. On September 5, 1951, the new Memorial Centre was officially opened, and a large granite plaque was dedicated to the memory of those who had served and those who had died in the Second World War.

Within a short period of time, a controversy erupted as to whether the Cenotaph should be moved to the Memorial Centre, placed in the City Hall Park or left on its original site in the front of the post office. Finally, a plebiscite was held to settle the issue with the majority of voters registering their opposition to any relocation.

While the community was resolving the issues of its war memorials, another war broke out in the spring of 1950 in Korea. A number of Central Albertans served during

this conflict in the Canadian units of the United Nations Forces, and three local men lost their lives overseas. However, over thirty-five years would pass before a public memorial to them would be erected.

A few months after Canada entered the Korean conflict, the local economy entered a brief recession. Construction activity slowed and the value of the building permits issued by the city declined by almost 40 percent. Farmers suffered poor harvests because of late frosts, bad hailstorms and an early onset of winter in October 1951. The local industrial development board reported that of eight major prospective business ventures, none had materialized.

Central Alberta's economy received a big boost, however, in mid-1951 when the Korean conflict and the broader cold war prompted the federal government to reactivate the Penhold Air Base as a North Atlantic Treaty Organization flying training school. Over the next two years millions of dollars worth of construction and improvements were carried out. Actual flight instruction began in July 1953, the same month as the cessation of hostilities in Korea.

There was also a major boost to the local economy with an increase in oil and gas exploration activity. Following the discovery of major oil fields in the Stettler–Big Valley areas in 1949 and 1950, seismograph crews became active in the Red Deer district. Later, drilling commenced both east and west of the city with major oil reefs being discovered west of Sylvan and Gull Lakes in 1952. In the summer of 1953, a major oil field was discovered a few miles northeast of Red Deer in the Joffre area. Eventually, there were nearly 300 wells producing in the region.

Red Deer was soon in the midst of another astounding boom. Between 1951 and 1954, the city's population rose from 7,575 to nearly 11,000 residents. Nearly 400 new homes and several new businesses were built with the value of building permits issued soaring to nearly $4 million per year. Important new industries were established including a brewery and electrical transformer, diamond drill, and egg-processing plants. Red Deer's importance as a regional distribution centre was enhanced by the construction of a major auto parts depot and several new warehouses.

As had been the case in the postwar boom, the city administration struggled to cope with the explosion of growth. Hundreds of thousands of dollars were spent on new utilities services and capital improvements. Because of a priority given to sewer and water main installations, road construction and paving lagged. With the wet climatic cycle continuing, the streets and lanes became virtual morasses. In 1954 city council made plans to construct an expensive storm sewer system to deal with the drainage problems. Ironically, it was also forced to build a new $430,000 water treatment plant in order to maintain an adequate domestic water supply.

The view from the old tower on Red Deer's City Hall in 1954, looking southwest toward the old Knox Presbyterian Church and Hospital Hill.

Utilities, roads and storm sewers were not the only challenges facing the community. By the early 1950s the Red Deer Athletic Association, which had been responsible for most of the city's sports programs and for the operation of the arena, found that its obligations had become too onerous for a volunteer organization. Consequently, city council, which had already been covering the salary of the association's sports director, agreed to establish a commission which would be responsible for all of the recreational activities in the community.

The aldermen also agreed to replace the 1925 arena building with a much larger and more modern facility. The old structure was demolished in the summer of 1951, and the site was sold to a national grocery chain in order to provide more money for the project. However, construction of the new building was unexpectedly delayed when the tenders received exceeded the budgeted funds by $80,000 and a sharp controversy arose over whether the arena should be located at the fairgrounds on the "outskirts of the city."

Eventually, a plebiscite was held to settle the dispute over the site and the necessary additional funding was secured. Work on the structure at the fairgrounds was finished in December 1952. After a mild spell

Ross Street, looking west, 1954. The mid-1950s were years of tremendous growth for the City of Red Deer.

and its ratepayers, the tremendous costs of these construction projects were eased somewhat when the provincial government increased its school building grants. However, this funding assistance was for classrooms and not administrative space. As a result, when a new facility for industrial arts and home economics instruction was built in 1953, a new board room, which doubled as a library and a small office for the secretary-treasurer, were included in the building.

In contrast to the public school district, the Red Deer School Division did not initially embark on a major construction program in the city. Instead it established an elementary and junior high school, Balmoral No. 3, in the old army huts next to the Composite High School. In 1953, however, a policy of centralizing rural schools was initiated, and increasing numbers of students were bussed in from outlying districts.

In 1954 the school division board built a new facility for the high school students. Most of the burgeoning junior grades were then moved into the old "Comp" buildings. Unfortunately, this collection of huts, which was renamed Riverglen, had become rather dilapidated with leaking roofs, buckled floors and broken water pipes being continual problems. Nevertheless, five years would pass before a new school building would be built.

The Red Deer Separate School District also turned to the old A–20 army camp for solutions to its problem of rapidly rising enrolments. In 1948 the Daughters of Wisdom purchased and moved an old army hut for use as a primary room and assembly hall. However, within two years all of their classrooms in the Convent and Montfort (old St. Mary's) schools were again badly overcrowded. In 1950 the separate school board decided to obtain additional space by purchasing its first school building, the old A–20 YMCA hut, on 58th Street.

Although this structure, renamed Sacred Heart School, had become rather ram-

delayed the official opening for a week, city council agreed to float another $80,000 debenture to pay for an artificial ice plant.

During the time that the arena project was being completed, the Red Deer Curling Club decided to replace its old rink on 52nd Street. Although the building had been renovated many times over the years, it had become somewhat rundown and was too small for many events such as the annual Farmers' Bonspiel, which had started in 1945. The club also decided to relocate to a spot next to the arena so that it would make use of the artificial ice plant. On July 13, 1953, Prime Minister Louis St. Laurent turned the first sod, and in January 1954 the new curling rink officially opened.

While the civic administration and sports organizations strove to meet the challenges of the rapidly changing community, the local school districts struggled to accommodate their escalating enrolments. Between 1950 and 1954, the public school board doubled its number of school buildings to ten, and every year either built a new school or made an addition to an existing one. In 1952 it built two new schools, South and South Hill, while in 1953 and 1954, it built two additions to Grandview School, which was then only three years old.

Fortunately, for the public school board

shackle and only had an old pot-bellied stove for heating, it was used for a number of years. Finally, in 1955 the school board replaced it with a new four-roomed schoolhouse that had a gymnasium. The trustees also built a similar-sized building, new Montfort, across the road from St. Joseph's Convent.

As the school boards and others focused their energies on current problems and future needs, the community as a whole increasingly reflected on its past. Annie L. Gaetz, with the sponsorship of the Quota Club, published a comprehensive history of Central Alberta. In 1951 the Old Timers' Association erected a cairn dedicated to the early pioneers at the Old Crossing. The provincial government agreed to designate the pristine Gaetz Lakes Sanctuary as a Provincial Wildlife Park. In 1954 a monument was unveiled north of the city in commemoration of the 200th anniversary of Anthony Henday's famous trip to Central Alberta.

The remembrance of the past reached a new height in 1955 when Alberta celebrated its Golden Jubilee as a province. A number of special events were held in Red Deer throughout the year to mark the anniversary. The main celebrations were held in early August as part of the annual Red Deer Fair, and more than 15,000 people turned out to watch the Jubilee parade. As well, the *Red Deer Advocate* produced a seventy-two page special edition, its largest ever, as a

souvenir of the occasion and as a documentation of the history of the city and district.

There was a profound pride in the community over the tremendous progress both the province and the city had made. However, there was also a feeling of nostalgia. This was not the same wistful recall of better times as had emerged during the Depression years. Instead it was a growing sense of loss as the new developments replaced familiar landmarks, and beautiful old buildings such as the Gaetz United Church were destroyed through the tragedy of fire. Moreover, although Red Deer had become a bustling, prosperous centre, the debt-free city of only ten years before now owed more than $2.5 million, the property tax rates were among the highest in the province and the new roads and services never seemed to be finished.

ABOVE: In 1954 the Red Deer School Division built a new high school and moved its students out of the old A–20 army huts. The new school was named Lindsay Thurber in honour of the local school inspector who had strongly advocated school consolidation.

BELOW: Red Deer's Mayor Harvey "Doc" Halladay handing a commemorative package of mail to the drivers of a rather fanciful replica of the old Calgary–Edmonton stagecoach, 1955.

ABOVE: The demolition of the old Michener Block, on the corner of Gaetz Avenue and 49th Street, was just one more indication of the rapid disappearance of old Red Deer during the boom years of the 1950s.

BELOW: The construction of the new Deerhome Institution in the late 1950s provided Red Deer with a renewed economic stimulus as the great boom began to flag. The spruce trees in the foreground are part of the Gaetz Lakes Sanctuary.

Regardless of any feelings of the residents, the great boom continued to surge ahead. In 1955 nearly $2 million worth of new housing was constructed. A residential development for senior citizens, which had been sponsored by the Kiwanis Club, opened and work began on Red Deer's first public facility for the care of the elderly, the Twilight Lodge. A new school was built in the Mountview area, and plans were announced for another junior high school on the southeastern outskirts of the city in the new Eastview subdivision.

The boom was bolstered by a surge in oil and gas exploration activity. After significant discoveries were made in the Burbank district in mid-1955, several oil companies bid $1.5 million for mineral rights leases around the city. Millions of dollars more were later spent for rights in other parts of Central Alberta. Soon dozens of new wells were drilled and began producing. Within the year ten new oil and oil-related companies started operations in Red Deer, while a number of others expanded their shops and offices. The petroleum service industry was rapidly becoming a major component of the local economy.

There were also important developments in the public sector. In 1955 the provincial government announced the construction of Deerhome, a new facility for the care of mentally handicapped adults, as well as further expansion of the existing Provincial Training School. Work on the multimillion-dollar project began almost immediately.

Despite the momentous plans for the two mental health care institutions as well as other popular initiatives such as the introduction of a five-mill education tax subsidy, the local fortunes of the governing Social Credit Party began to wane. Earlier political upheavals had come during times of war or economic depression, but now the changes wrought by the prolonged boom seemed to cause another shift in allegiances. In 1954 the opposition Progressive Conservative Party candidate, W.J. Kirby, scored an upset in a provincial by-election, and in 1955 he triumphed again in the general election.

Three years later Social Credit suffered another reversal when it lost the federal riding of Red Deer for the first time in twenty-three years.

As the city entered the latter part of the 1950s, the local economy suffered some setbacks. The value of new construction dropped by 30 percent in 1956–57 and would have fallen even further without the massive Deerhome projects. The crown-owned Polymer Corporation announced plans to build a multimillion-dollar synthetic rubber plant, but the proposal never progressed past the purchase of a 400-hectare site northeast of the city.

There were problems in the Joffre oil fields. The output of the wells started to decline because of a drop in gas pressure. In 1957 the oil companies managed to restore their production levels by one of the first applications in Canada of the water injection method of enhanced oil recovery.

By late 1957 the economy of Central Alberta began to rebound and quickly soared to new heights. Before the end of the decade, nearly $14 million worth of construction was started, including four new schools, eleven new churches and yet another major addition to the Red Deer General Hospital. Red Deer's population grew by an average of 7 percent per year, but in 1958 it rose by a phenomenal 21 percent to 16,500. Half of this latter increase was attributable to the expansion of the physical size of the city from eleven to thirty-three square kilometres. Nevertheless, Red Deer had gained the distinction of being the fastest-growing city in Canada.

The enormous enlargement of the municipal boundaries in 1958 was prompted by a desire to accommodate and control the incredible growth in the community. It also allowed the city's officials to continue the practice, started in 1948, of purchasing blocks of land for future development. This land-banking scheme was financed with the proceeds from lot sales. Moreover, in order

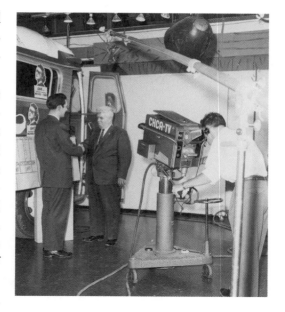

A joint CNIB–Lions Club fund-raiser staged in the studios of the new local television station CHCA–TV. The show was held the same night as the civic elections, hence the vote-total board on the left of the photograph.

to minimize the costs of servicing the new residential subdivisions, a prepayment system was instituted for services and improvements. Despite these measures the city was still faced with enormous capital costs. By 1960 the level of municipal debt had rise to more than $6 million.

As the record-setting boom continued to grow in strength, the community enjoyed a number of notable and unique advances. In the fall of 1957 Red Deer became the first place in Alberta to introduce artificial fluoridation of water. The following year the city built what was purported to be the world's largest spheroid water reservoir. To many the "green onion" became a symbol of the community. In 1959 AGT began extensive improvements to the telephone service, including the construction of a new three-storey exchange building. Two years later the first direct distance dialling system in Western Canada went into operation in Red Deer.

There were other locally important developments. In October 1957 the Old Timers' Association turned the sod for a log pioneer's lodge next to the fairgrounds. The following month the era of television arrived in Red Deer when station CHCA began broadcasting. The Deerhome facility was opened for residents on January 8, 1958.

The new Plaza Shopping Centre and Co-op store were built on the grounds of the old CNR station, which had been relocated to North Red Deer in 1961.

Within two years there were more than 1,500 residents in the two mental institutions, and the number of new jobs at the complex rose accordingly. In 1959 Red Deer's first shopping centres opened, one in West Park and then another in the Eastview subdivision. Shortly thereafter city council, after a great deal of debate, passed a bylaw regulating shopping hours. Stores were allowed to open on Thursday evenings with Wednesday afternoons being declared as retail half-holidays.

There were changes in the sphere of politics. The local Social Credit Party regained some of the strength it had lost. In 1959 it recaptured the provincial constituency from the Progressive Conservatives, and three years later the national party leader, Robert Thompson, won back the federal riding. However, the contests were close, particularly in Red Deer's urban polls, where the Tories remained a strong alternative to the Socreds.

Not all of the developments in local politics were contentious. In 1959 Mrs. Margaret Parsons became the first woman to hold the position of chairman of the public school board. Two years later the citizens of Red Deer elected their first woman alderman, Mrs. Ethel Taylor.

As the 1950s drew to a close and another decade arrived, a new era emerged in the realm of transportation. The provincial government completed its new four-laned highway between Calgary and Edmonton. Although a bypass was constructed to the west of the city, Red Deer's role as a regional distribution centre was greatly enhanced by the resulting increase in motorized freight and traffic. As well, most residents welcomed the reduction in the terrible congestion which had existed on Gaetz Avenue.

In 1959 the CNR decided to move its rail yards from the south side of the river. Ever since CN's troublesome bridge across the Red Deer River had been abandoned in 1941, the use of the station on Ross Street had become increasingly impractical. In 1960 work began on a new terminal and yards on the east side of Gaetz Avenue in North Red Deer. The city developed the adjoining property into an industrial park which quickly attracted a number of new warehouses and shops.

The relocation of the CNR meant that a great deal of land on the south and eastern edges of the downtown core was available for redevelopment. The right-of-way north of 55th Street had already been turned into a residential area in the late 1940s. In 1962 a large new shopping mall was built on the old CN station grounds. The area south of

49th Street was largely turned into parkland, but the city decided to build a large new recreation centre on a parcel near 45th Street. An indoor swimming pool was included in the complex, and two years later, in 1964, the city built another Olympic-sized outdoor pool alongside the building. The old 1949 pool was sold and replaced with a commercial building.

There was also some redevelopment alongside the old railroad right-of-way. In 1961 the Nazarene Church closed its college on the southwestern edge of the transfer track between the CNR and CPR lines. The students were transferred to a new institution in Winnipeg, the old campus grounds were sold and the site was later redeveloped into another large shopping plaza.

At the same time as the Nazarene College shut its doors, the Red Deer School Division decided to close its high school dormitories. The old army huts had finally become so dilapidated that they would have to be replaced, but with so many rural students now using daily buses, the board did not feel that such an expense would be justified. As well, because a high proportion of the enrolment at the high school was now from the city, the school division decided to transfer the "Comp" to the public school district. The cost was set at a token one dollar, but the public board also agreed to assume all of the outstanding indebtedness on the building.

A few months after the change in responsibility for the Composite High School, the Red Deer public school board began the construction of a vocational high school with extensive funding from the federal government. This new facility provided technical and commercial training as well as senior academic instruction. Industrial arts classes for high school students continued to be taught at the adjacent "Comp" with one of the A–20 drill halls still serving as the shops.

After the construction of the new Riverglen School in 1960, the Red Deer Separate School District moved its senior grades from St. Joseph's Convent to the old barrack school. However, as the Red Deer School Division had discovered, the buildings were rapidly reaching the point where they could no longer be safely used. In 1962 the Catholic school board built a new junior and senior high school next to the Maryview School on 39th Street. In that same year, the Daughters of Wisdom decided that a dormitory was no longer needed and the convent boarding school was closed.

While the various educational authorities were making changes to their school accommodations, the local municipal officials sought improvements to their increasingly inadequate administrative facilities. In 1961 the MD of Red Deer constructed a new building on 32nd Street. Although the Red Deer School Division also moved its offices into this structure, it was not until January 1963 that the two jurisdictions amalgamated to form the County of Red Deer.

In the fall of 1961, the City of Red Deer erected a new public works building west of the CPR tracks. Consideration was also given to the construction of a new administration building on 52nd Street, but the idea was dropped after loud protests from groups such as the local chamber of commerce. In the spring of 1962 the city's officials were able to relieve some of the serious overcrowding problem in the City Hall by moving the Fire Department into the adjacent Armoury. Ironically, this structure had been seriously damaged in a blaze shortly after it had been acquired by the city from the Department of National Defence.

During 1962 city council finally decided that it was no longer reasonable to make do with the old City Hall building. In late November the first sod was turned for a new edifice. The aldermen were shocked when the tenders came in at $200,000 more than the original estimates. However, after much cutting of "frills," the city staff managed to reduce the cost of the project to a

ABOVE: An architect's model of Red Deer's new City Hall preceded the construction in 1964 of this striking but often controversial building.

BELOW: A view of Red Deer's City Hall and City Hall Park taken in 1966 when Red Deer became the fourth largest city in Alberta. The new six-storey Professional Building appears on the left of the photograph.

to the memory of the first mayor, F.W. Galbraith, while the *Red Deer Advocate* published a souvenir fifty-page edition of the paper. Although a proposal to create a museum in the old Indian Industrial School was never carried out, within a year Alberta's first municipal archives was opened in a small room in the new City Hall.

The ebullience of the celebrations reflected the fact that the golden anniversary occurred as the great boom reached its peak. There was a new surge of activity in the petroleum industry, and the flares of nearly 1,500 oil and gas wells in Central Alberta were signals of prosperity. The local farmers were in the midst of a seven-year streak of bumper crops with good prices for their produce. The value of new construction soared to nearly $11 million and included three new schools, an auxiliary care hospital, a tourist centre and a meat packing plant. New subdivisions mushroomed not only on the southeastern edges of the community, but also in North Red Deer. The 1963 civic census figure of 23,106, up nearly 10 percent in one year, confirmed that Red Deer was still the fastest growing city in Canada.

As the golden year drew to a close, the local economy received a major blow when the federal government decided not to have jet training at the Penhold air base. Although the NORAD (North American Air Defence Agreement) radar installation, which had been built in the early 1960s, remained operational and a RCMP training centre temporarily replaced the flying school, the base was soon reduced to a fraction of its former size.

As the decade progressed, the great boom rapidly began to lose steam. Residential construction dropped by 50 percent in 1964 and the total value of new construction dropped by over $4 million in two years. Although Red Deer achieved the status of being Alberta's fourth largest city in 1966, the rate of population increase had slowed

more acceptable sum without significantly altering the external appearance of the building.

On March 25, 1963, the official cornerstone of the new City Hall was unveiled, a ceremony which was particularly auspicious as it took place on the fiftieth anniversary of Red Deer's incorporation as a city. A number of other special events and festivities were held to mark the civic Golden Jubilee. There was a massive parade through the downtown area, and fifty people walked fifty miles (eighty kilometres) from the neighbouring town of Rocky Mountain House. A four-hectare park was dedicated

to 2 percent per year or almost one-fifth of what it had been at the height of the boom.

There were many indications of the economic slowdown. The local brewery closed and the Polymer Corporation finally decided to sell off its rubber plant site. A $4-million hotel and shopping centre complex was proposed for the downtown area, but the plans were soon abandoned.

This is not to suggest that there were no significant developments in the community. While Red Deer was not growing as fast as it had been, it was still progressing. In 1964 the Red Deer Junior College, a long-standing dream of the community, opened in temporary quarters in the Lindsay Thurber Composite High School. Two private nursing homes were constructed, one in West Park and the other in the South Hill area. The public school board built three more schools in three years. An extensive athletic park was developed by the city in North Red Deer, and a second traffic bridge was built across the Red Deer River. The city was able to lease part of the Penhold base as a municipal airport, and a holiday trailer manufacturing plant opened on 67th Street.

In 1967 Red Deer reached another historical benchmark when it celebrated Canada's centennial year. Of special honour to the community was the appointment of a "hometown boy" Roland Michener to the position of Governor General. There was tremendous excitement in November when Mr. Michener and his wife, Norah, made a vice-regal visit to Red Deer. He officially opened the new public library, Red Deer's centennial project, and dedicated the Junior College complex, which was under construction on the south side of the city.

Mr. Michener had an easy style with people. His quick wit and sense of humour quickly dispelled any notions of a Governor General as a stuffy, reserved autocrat. Many in the city were also astonished to see the athletic Michener out jogging in the early morning when others half his age were still in bed. A strong affection for the Micheners developed in the community, and a warm welcome was extended to them during each of their future visits.

The Centennial was not only memorable as a year of celebration. It also marked the start of a modest economic upturn for the community. Although there was not the return to the wild growth of earlier years, the pace of new development quickened. A railcar repair facility and two meat packing plants opened in the Riverside Industrial Park, and a can factory was built alongside the CPR line near 53rd Street. The public

LEFT: Roland Michener, sometimes affectionately referred to as Canada's jogging Governor General, quickly won the hearts of Red Deer's citizens when he made a return trip to his hometown shortly after his vice-regal appointment in 1967.

RIGHT: The construction of Red Deer College in 1967 marked a major advance in the educational opportunities available in Central Alberta.

Personal Covenant of

R. N. Thompson

Social Credit Candidate for the
Constituency of

RED DEER

I hereby affirm to the electors of my
Constituency that I subscribe unreservedly
to the Statement of Social Credit National
Policy contained herein and, if elected, will
strive to the utmost of my ability to ensure
its implementation.

R. N. Thompson

On April 8 VOTE
SOCIAL CREDIT

THOMPSON, ROBERT N. | X

Published by the Red Deer Social Credit Constituency Association
Printed by Bradburn Printers Ltd., 10455 - 95 Street, Edmonton

*The Time
Has Come*

**TO INSURE
CANADA'S
FUTURE**

With A
*National
Social Credit
Policy*

Robert Thompson, Red Deer's Member of Parliament and national leader of the Social Credit Party, created a country-wide controversy when he switched to the Progressive Conservative Party. Although the subsequent election in Red Deer was hard-fought, Thompson easily retained his seat.

national Liberal Party, Mr. Thompson was reelected by a comfortable margin.

If Red Deer's political affiliations had not changed very much, there was a strong indication of the more cosmopolitan make-up of the community when the first International Folk Festival was held in the early summer of 1969. An estimated 60,000 people took in the various ethnic pavilions and entertainments. The whole event was such a phenomenal success that the festival subsequently became the main focus of Red Deer's annual Canada Day celebrations.

While Red Deer's multicultural groups had enjoyed a triumph, the local agricultural community was beset by hard times. The great grain bonanza of the 1960s had come to an end as markets shrank and prices declined. By 1970 the economy of Central Alberta was in recession. Construction activity slowed to a crawl and the population of the city dropped for the first time in forty years.

The outlook seemed bleak, but the economy had reached its nadir. For the rest of the decade conditions began to improve, slowly at first and then at an accelerated rate. One of the first major signs of a turnaround came with the construction on the North Hill of Red Deer's first full-scale shopping mall. Another indication was the erection of Red Deer's first five-storey office building on the corner of Ross Street and Gaetz Avenue.

During the summer of 1971 there was a profound change in Alberta's politics. After thirty-six consecutive years of power, the Social Credit government was toppled and replaced with a Progressive Conservative administration. Social Credit lingered on as a political force in Central Alberta and even came close in 1979 to recapturing the Red Deer constituency, which it had lost eight years before. However, the party was generally in serious decline, both locally and across the province, and eventually disappeared from the political landscape.

school board built a new junior high school in West Park, while the separate school board constructed the Camille J. Lerouge Collegiate near the Composite High School. A third floor was added to the hospital in 1968, and during the following year the hospital board began construction of a new nursing home in Fairview. In three years nearly 450 new housing starts were recorded.

There were some interesting developments in the realm of politics as well. In 1968 Robert Thompson switched from the Social Credit to the Progressive Conservative Party, and many local Tories had trouble accepting their old rival as their candidate in the general election. Moreover, the local political turmoil was intensified when an unknown assailant fired shots at the local Liberal candidate. Nevertheless, while the country was swept up by a political phenomenon dubbed "Trudeaumania," which resulted in a landslide victory for the

Within two years of the change in government, a new era emerged for the Deerhome Institute and the Provincial Training School, which had been renamed Alberta School Hospital in 1965. Following the recommendations of the Blair Report, new policies were adopted including an emphasis on the integration of the mentally handicapped into the community. A program of deinstitutionalization was started to significantly reduce the resident population. In April 1973 the two institutions were amalgamated under one administration, and a major reconstruction of the facilities was carried out. In 1977, after a new recreation complex was completed, the institution was renamed Michener Centre in honour of the former Governor General.

Meanwhile, in late 1973 the international OPEC cartel forced a dramatic increase in world oil prices. An incredible surge in local natural gas and oil activity quickly followed. Dozens of new wells were drilled and a great many new service companies started operations in the city.

In 1974 an announcement was made that a multimillion-dollar ethylene plant would be built northeast of Red Deer as the first stage in the development of a world-scale, natural-gas based petrochemical industry in Central Alberta. As work on the massive project proceeded, the brilliant flares of the plant site became a beacon to an prosperous future.

The extent of the new boom was staggering. The population of Red Deer jumped from 30,000 in 1975 to more than 46,000 in 1981. Building activity skyrocketed to nearly $140 million per year, or almost twice the amount which had been invested in all of the 1960s. New manufacturing plants, office towers, shopping malls, hotels, apartment blocks and other commercial buildings sprang up all over the city, while hundreds of new homes were built in the burgeoning new subdivisions.

Most of the new growth was concentrated on the north side of the Red Deer, so

that by the early 1980s, 40 percent of the city's residents lived north of the river. In order to provide recreational and educational services to many of these citizens, the civic administration joined with the public and separate school districts to build an unique complex, the G.H. Dawe Community Centre, which included a public community school, library, swimming pool, arena and a Catholic school, St. Patrick's.

Numerous other public facilities were constructed. A senior citizen's drop-in centre, the Golden Circle, was built on the old CNR right-of-way near 46th Street. The Red Deer Museum, the city's Diamond Jubilee project, moved with the Archives into a new facility on an adjacent site. The provincial government built a multimillion-dollar office complex on 51st Street. A massive new Regional Hospital Centre was con-

ABOVE: The moving of the Cronquist house in March 1976 from West Park to Bower Ponds in North Red Deer drew a tremendous amount of public attention. The house subsequently became the headquarters for the Red Deer International Folk Festival Society.

BELOW: The new multi-million dollar Red Deer Regional Hospital Centre reflected not only the tremendous growth of the city in the 1970s and early 1980s, but also its growing role as a major regional centre.

The boom of the 1970s and early 1980s marked yet another massive transformation of the city's downtown area and the further disappearance of most of old Red Deer.

structed alongside the old General and Auxiliary hospitals. The public library had another floor added to it, while the City Hall gained another two storeys. Two new fire halls were erected on 67th and 32nd Streets and a new traffic bridge was built across the river west of the CPR tracks.

A highlight of the boom years came in 1980 when Alberta celebrated its 75th anniversary as a province. The provincial government allocated $75 million for the celebrations with the proviso that the funds were not to be used for capital projects. Red Deer's share of this largesse amounted to $800,000, most of which was spent on a variety of special events as well as a set of modern metal sculptures and a pictorial history book of the city, *Proud Beginnings*. The remainder of the money was placed in a special fund for future community heritage projects.

As had been the case with Red Deer's Golden Jubilee, the Provincial 75th Anniversary occurred at the climax of the boom. New federal energy policies in 1980–81 followed by a sharp decline in world petroleum prices in 1982–83 sent the local economy into recession. The onset of the slump was delayed somewhat by the momentum of the great boom, buttressed by such major projects as the construction of two major manufacturing plants, further petrochemical developments in the Joffre and Prentiss areas and the relocation of the Westerner Exposition to new fairgrounds on the south side of the city. Nevertheless, by 1984 Red Deer's growth rate had plunged to less than one fifth of what it had been in 1981.

In the early 1980s the City of Red Deer developed the beautiful Waskasoo Park system with the financial assistance of the provincial government. The old Allen bungalow, shown here when it was owned by the Busby family in the 1940s, was restored and became the residence for the park naturalist.

A slow recovery emerged in the mid-1980s with the rate of population increase creeping back up to a modest 3 percent per year. A major advance for the city during that time was the development of the Waskasoo Park along the Red Deer River and tributary creeks. Extensive networks of hiking and bicycling paths were created, and a coordinated series of new recreational facilities were constructed at various points along the park corridor. In 1985 the centenary of the Riel Rebellion, the new Fort Normandeau Interpretive Centre was built at the Old Crossing. In 1986 the Kerry Wood Nature Centre, which had been named for Red Deer's renowned author and naturalist, opened next to the Gaetz Lakes Sanctuary.

In 1988 Red Deer marked the 75th anniversary of its incorporation as a city. One of the most important events in the celebration of this civic birthday was the dedication of Heritage Square, within Rotary Recreation Park, south of the Museum and Archives building. Along the perimeters of this picturesque place were the Norwegian Society's cultural centre, the Aspelund Laft Hus, as well as the former library annex to Reverend Leonard Gaetz's retirement home, the steeple from the old Knox Presbyterian Church, a replica of the

The old Presbyterian Church steeple became one of the main features of Heritage Square, a collection of historical buildings next to the Red Deer Museum and Archives. The Square was officially dedicated in 1988 as part of the 75th anniversary celebrations of Red Deer's incorporation as a city.

1887 log schoolhouse and Red Deer's oldest surviving building, the tiny Stevenson-Hall Block, which had stood on the corner of Ross Street and Gaetz Avenue in the early 1890s.

These modest historical structures in their peaceful park setting stood in marked contrast to the bustling modern city which surrounded them. They provided a visible measure of how much Red Deer had changed in its many decades of development.

ABOVE: The old armoury, which had become Red Deer's Fire Hall in 1961, was reconverted into the Children's Library wing for the Red Deer Public Library in 1995. This was the last major public project completed during the "cut-back" years of the early 1990s.

RIGHT: The City of Red Deer as it appeared in an aerial photograph in October 1995.

to the city's prosperity was still the fertile parklands with their bountiful resources. The weather always seemed both capricious and unprecedented.

Nevertheless, the pristine wilderness had been turned into a mixed agricultural heartland. The frontier settlement had been displaced by a thriving town. The modest parkland community had been transformed into a modern urban centre of more than 60,000 residents. Red Deer might still be a point on the map, but it was also now one of the most important localities in Western Canada.

In looking back on the years of change and development with the various booms, depressions, wars, eras of peace, triumphs, tragedies and all of the other historical events and personalities, one is struck by the richness of Red Deer's past. At the same time one can only wonder at the future.

The existence of this "museum of buildings" also reflected the fact that most of the old Red Deer had been displaced by the new.

There were some things about the community which had not varied. Red Deer remained a central point on the major transportation routes of Alberta. The key

Bibliography

Batchelor, Bruce Edward. *The Agrarian Frontier Near Red Deer and Lacombe, Alberta, 1882-1914.* Vancouver: Simon Fraser University, 1978.

Belanger, Art. *The Calgary–Edmonton, Edmonton–Calgary Trail.* Calgary: Frontier Publishing, 1983.

Blue, John. *Alberta Past and Present.* Chicago: Pioneer Historical Publishing, 1924.

Burnt Lake History Society. *Along the Burnt Lake Trail.* Calgary: Friesen Printers, 1977.

Dawe, Wellington. *History of Red Deer.* Red Deer: Kiwanis Club, 1967.

Dawe, Wellington. *The Story of Fort Normandeau.* Red Deer: Fort Normandeau Restoration Committee, 1975.

Dempsey, Hugh A. *Indian Tribes of Alberta.* Calgary: Glenbow Alberta Institute, 1974.

Dempsey, Hugh A. *The Rundle Journals, 1840-1848.* Calgary: Historical Society of Alberta, 1977.

Gaetz, Annie L. *Footprints of The Gaetz Family.* Red Deer: A.L. Gaetz, 1953.

Gaetz, Annie L. *The Park Country.* Vancouver: Evergreen Press, 1948.

Gaetz, Annie L. *Trails of Yesterday.* Red Deer: A.L. Gaetz, 1952.

Gaetz, L.L. (Dick). *The Family Story.* Calgary: L.L. Gaetz, 1978.

Gaetz Memorial United Church. *A Journey in Faith, 1887-1987.* Red Deer: Fletcher Printing Co., 1987.

Grove, Dave. *The Puck and I in Red Deer.* Red Deer: Adviser Publications, n.d.

Helgason, Gail. *The First Albertans.* Edmonton: Lone Pine Publishing, 1987.

Kerr, John R. *Other Days and Other Ways.* Red Deer: J.R. Kerr, 1952.

MacGregor, James G. *A History of Alberta.* Edmonton: Hurtig Publishers, 1975.

MacGregor, James G. *The Battle River Valley.* Saskatoon: Western Producer Prairie Books, 1976.

MacGregor, James G. *Father Lacombe.* Edmonton: Hurtig Publishers, 1975.

MacGregor, James G. *Behold the Shining Mountains.* Edmonton: Applied Arts Products, 1954.

Maclean, John. *McDougall of Alberta.* Toronto: Ryerson Press, 1927.

Marsh, James H., Editor. *The Canadian Encyclopedia.* Edmonton: Hurtig Publishers, 1988.

McRae, A.O. *History of the Province of Alberta.* Calgary: Western Canada History Co., 1912.

Meeres, E.L. *Homesteads that Nurtured a City.* Red Deer: Red Deer and District Museum Society, 1984.

Moore, John T. *The Settlers Pocket Guide To Homesteads in the Canadian Northwest.* Toronto: Saskatchewan Land and Homestead Company, 1884.

Morrison, Bruce and Wilson, Roderick. *Native Peoples, The Canadian Experience.* Toronto: McClelland and Stewart, 1986.

North Red Deer 75th Anniversary Committee. *The Little Village That Grew.* Red Deer: Adviser Graphics, 1987.

Parker, Georgean C. *Proud Beginnings: A Pictorial History of Red Deer.* Red Deer: Red Deer and District Museum Society, 1981.

Parsons, Dr. W.B. *A History of the Rotary Club of Red Deer 1923-1973.* Red Deer: Royell Reproductions, 1973.

Poplar Ridge Historical Committee. *The Districts' Diary.* Calgary: Friesen Printers, 1981.

Prud 'homme, Essie. *Yesteryears of the Hays Municipality.* Red Deer: County of Red Deer No. 23, 1967.

Red Deer Advocate. *Red Deer: Red Deer Advocate Ltd., 1904-1989.*

Red Deer and District Local No. 24. *ATA Schools of the Parkland.* Red Deer: Local No. 24 ATA, 1967.

Red Deer East Historical Society. *Mingling Memories.* Calgary: Friesen Printers, 1979.

Red Deer News. *Red Deer: News Publishing Co., 1906-1926.*

Snell, Harold. *History of Red Deer Lodge #12, G.R.A. AF and AM.* Red Deer: Advocate Press, 1924.

Stalker, A.M. *Surficial Geology of the Red Deer-Stettler Map-Area, Alberta.* Ottawa: Geological Survey of Canada, 1960.

Stewart, Norman. *Children of the Pioneers.* Calgary: Foothills Printers, 1962.

Thomson, Dorothy J. *A Vine of His Planting: History of Canadian Nazarene College.* Edmonton: Commercial Printers, 1961.

Wood, Kerry. *A Corner of Canada.* Calgary: John A. McAra, 1967.

Wood, Kerry. *Red Deer: A Love Story.* Red Deer: Advocate Printers, 1975.

Wood, Kerry. *The Sanctuary.* Edmonton: Hamly Press, 1952.

Wood, Kerry. *The Map-maker: The Story of David Thompson.* Toronto: MacMillan Co., 1955.

Wood, Kerry. *Mickey the Beaver and Other Stories.* Toronto: MacMillan Co., 1964.

Wood, Kerry. *The Great Chief.* Toronto: MacMillan Co. 1960.

Index

Italics indicate illustrations

75th Anniversary (provincial) 154
75th Anniversary (civic) 155
31st Battalion 95
63rd Battalion 72
66th Battalion 72
89th Battalion 72, 73
187th Battalion 73, 77
191st Battalion 77
12th Canadian Mounted Rifles (CMR) 69
35th Central Alberta Horse 67
23rd Field Battery 116
78th Field Battery 94, 116, 118, 121
92nd Field Battery 116

A–20 Camp 119–121, 131, 132, 142, 144
Aberhart, William 109, 110, 117, 129
Aboriginal Peoples 15–23
Alberta Advocate (newspaper) 54
Alberta and Athabasca Railway Company 39
Alberta Central Railroad (ACR) 58, 63, 65
Alberta Government Telephones (AGT) 52, 91, 147
Alberta Hotel 44, 47, 74
Alberta Ladies College 61, 76, 90, 98
Alberta Lumber Company 38–39
Alberta Mounted Rifles 36
Alberta Natural History Society (ANHS) 96
Alberta Pacific Grain Company 88, *88*, 101
Alberta Provincial Police 80, 107
Alberta School Hospital 153
Alberta Veterans Volunteer Reserve 118
Alberta Wheat Pool 101
Aldous, Montague 27
Alexandra Club 81
Alexandra Hotel 50, 74
Alexandra Park 53, 60
Allen house, *155*
Allsop, S.J. 141
Anglican Parish Hall 90
Arlington Hotel 54, 74
Armistice 84
Aspelund Laft Hus 155
Atlas Lumber Company 98
Automobiles 60, 80, 88, 101, 111, 124
Aviation *83*, 87, 88, 104, 112, 124

Bailey, Frank *127*
Bannerman, Sage 31, 37
Baptist Church 53
Bawtinheimer, G.H. 55
Bawtinheimer Sawmill 55, *57*
Bearchell, Sid *127*
Beatty brothers 101
Beatty, George 29

Beatty, Jim 29
Beddington, Fred *127*
Bell, George 61
Bell, William 46
Bell Telephone 51
Bemister, George 42
Blackfoot Legend 9
Boer War 50
Borden, Robert 78
Botterill, Lois 99
Boy Scouts 61, *61*, 62
Bredin, W.F. 29

C & E Townsite Company 91–92
CHCA (television) 147
CKLC (radio) *100*, 101, 107, 141
CKRD (radio) 141
Calgary and Edmonton (C & E) Railway Company 39, 43, 47
Calgary–Edmonton Trail 26, 30, 35, 39, 43, 104
Calgary Highlanders 116
Calgary Power Ltd. 100
Calgary Tank Regiment 117, 121, 125
Camille J. Lerouge Collegiate 152
Canadian Army Band *127*
Canadian National Railroad 88–89, 92, 97, 101, 148
Canadian Northern Railroad (CNR) 58, 63, 70, 76–77
Canadian Northern Western Railroad (CNWR) 59, 63, 65
Canadian Pacific Railroad (CPR) 27, 30, 43, 56, 58, 63, 65, 77, 98, 105
Canadian Women's Army Corps 123
Capitol Theatre 112
Carlyle, D.R. 141
Cenotaph (war memnorial) 93–94, *94*, *133*, 141–142
Central Alberta Dairy Pool (CADP) 97, 110, 122
Central Alberta Dairy Pool Condensery *109*, 110
Central Alberta Oil Company 64
Central United Airways 104
Charbonneau, M.J. 31
Chautauqua 80, *81*
City Council 63
City Hall 149, *150*, 150, 154
City Hall Park *104*, 141, *141*
Clark, Michael 78
Collins, M.P. 30
Commercial Cafe 69
Conscription 78–79, 81, 118, 125
Coronation Park 110
Coryell, Lieutenant 35
Council of Women 81
Crescent Theatre 101
Cronquist House *153*
Cruickshanks, Charles 50

D.S. Long Harness Shop 81
Daughers of the Wisdom 55, 61, 90, 101, 149
de Smet, Father Pierre 20
Deerford, plan of 32
Deerhome 146, 147, 153
Dell, Irene 99
Dench Cartage Company 105
Denovan, Henrietta 51
Denovan, Howard 51
Dominion Elevator Company 46
Dominion Lands Agent 33, 47
Dominion Lands Surveyor(s) 27, 31
Dominion Lands Titles Office 80
Drought 105, 111, 128
Duncan, Margaret 46
Dunham, Matt 122

E.B. Eddy Company 103, 141
Earl of Bessborough 110
Eastern Star 81
Electrical Protection Act 99
Elks Club 99, 128 131
Elks Hall 108
Empress Theatre 95, 101
Epidemics 16, 20, 22, 83–84
Erasmus, Peter 21
Exhibition Park 69

Farmers Bonspiel 144
Farmers Cooperative Marketing Association 97
Fathers of St. Mary of Tinchebray 55, 90
Fidler, Peter 19
Fires 44, 53, 57, 101, 105, 124
Fisher, Walter *127*
Floods 48, 70, *70*, 105, *126*, 128, 137
Forbes, Doris 128, *128*
Forbes, Wallace 129
Fort Normandeau *25*, 35, 36, 37, 112, *112*
Fort Normandeau Interpretive Centre 155
Freytag Tannery Company 60

G.H. Dawe Community Centre 153
Gaetz Avenue *102*, *113*
Gaetz Cornett Drug and Bookstore 69
Gaetz Lakes Sanctuary 145, 155
Gaetz Manufacturing Company 60, 80
Gaetz United Church 61, *105*, 145
Gaetz, Annie L. 145
Gaetz, H.H. 60
Gaetz, Issac 37
Gaetz, John Jost 39
Gaetz, Leonard 10, 33, *33*, 36, 38, 39, 41, *41*, 44, 61, 155
Gaetz, Raymond 33, 49, 108
Gaetz, Tom 108
Galbraith, F.W. 64, 109, 150
George, Dr. Henry 83, 96
Gerard, Horace 123
Golden Circle 153

Golden Jubilee 109, 145, 150
Gorman, George 87
Grandview School 144
Great Chief Park 21
Great Depression 105–107, 109
Great War Veterans Association (GWVA) 81, 90, 95
Great West Lumber Company 55, 60,70, 80
Greenback, Fraser 127
Greene, George 44

H.H. Gaetz Block 50
Halladay, H.W. 136
Hayhoe, Helen 99
Henday, Anthony 19
Heritage Square 155
Hilsabeck, Fred 125
Hilsabeck, Jim 125
HMCS *Red Deer* 122, 122–123
Homestead Policy 27
Homesteaders 47
Hooey, Cliff 125
Horn, Maude 96
Hosak, Frank 127
Houston, Vera 99
Hudson's Bay Company 15, 16, 18, 19, 23
Huestis, Jessie 96

Imperial Oil Company 135
Indian Industrial School 43, 43, 44, 48, 91, 150
Influenza 83–84
International Folk Festival 152
International Order of the Daughters of the Empire (IODE) 81
Irish, Laura 96

Jenkins, Angus 50
Jessup, J.G. 47

Kains, Thomas 31
Karsh, Bernie 127
Kelly, Arthur 61
Kemp, William 29, 38
Kenny Farms Agency 88
Kerry Wood Nature Centre 155
King Edward VIII 110
King, G.C. 30, 33
King George V 110
King George VI 110, 113
King, MacKenzie 117
Kinsmen Club 111, 118
Kirby, W.J. 146
Kitching, Dorothy 99
Kiwanis Club 146
Klu Klux Klan 106, 106
Knights of Columbus 122, 123, 131
Knox Presbyterian Church 155
Korean War 142–143
Kosler, Frank 127

Lacombe, Father Albert 20, 20
Land Division Policy 27, 31
Laurentia Milk Company 60, 68
Laurier, Sir Wilfrid 58
Leacock, Stephen 109
Leduc 135
Lee, Scotty 99
Leeson and Scott Stagecoach 31
Lennie, Mary 33
Lennie, Thomas 33
Lindsay Thurber Comprehensive High School 145, 145, 149
Lions Club 111
Little, Jack 29, 33
Long, Ben 122
Lord Byng 94
Lord Strathcona 51
Lord Tweedsmuir 110–111
Love, George 54
Lynass, Tommy 127
Lyric Theatre 69

Macdonald, Brigadier General 88
MacKenzie, William 58
Maloney, J.J. 106
Mann, Donald 58
Manning, Ernest 110, 129
Manning–Sutherland Lumber Company 80
Maskepetoon 21, 21
Maskepetoon Park 21
Masonic Lodge 47, 72
Mathieson, Reverand E.K. 37
McClellan, Robert W. 25, 29, 29, 35, 36, 37, 38
McClellan, Sarah 29
McCreight, Edith 96
McDonald's Consolidated 108
McDougall, George 21 21
McDougall, John 21, 21
McGillis, Burnam (Bonhomme) 29, 34
McKenzie brothers 38, 45
McKenzie family 30, 30
McKenzie, R.A. 37
McNichol, Archibald 50
McPherson, Addison 25, 26–27, 29, 34
McQueen, Reverand Dr. 47
Meeres, Horace 53
Memorial Centre 141–142
Memorial Centre Committee 139, 141
Memorial Committee 94
Methodist Church 44
Methodist Missionary Society 28
Métis 22, 30, 33–34
Meyer, Henry 29
Michener Block 53
Michener Centre 153
Michener, Edward 52, 64, 74, 82
Michener, Norah 151
Michener, Roland 151, 151

Mickey the Beaver 128, 129
Mickleson, Ole 46
Military Services Act *see conscription*
Militia Training Centre *see A–20 camp*
Mission School 37, 44
Missionaries 20
Moore, John T. 28, 29, 33, 51
Mowat, John 34
Murphy, D.H. 44

National Fence Company 105
National Grain Company 101
National War Loan Campaign 119
Nazarene's Northern Bible School 103, 149
Neilly, William 37
Nelson, Gus 125
Nichols, Evelyn 99
Norbury, Frank 94
Normandeau, J.E. Bedard 35, 35
North Cottage School 61, 61
North Red Deer 56, 59–60, 111, 120, 137
North West Company 15, 19
North West Mounted Police (NWMP) 22, 36, 43
Northwest Entomological Society 47
Northwestern Utilities 124, 132, 136–137
Norwegian Society 155

Oil and gas industry 64, 65, 111, 143, 146, 150, 153
Old Timers Association 108, 109, 112
Olympia Cafe 69
Orange Hall 55
Our Lady of Sorrows Church 55

Palliser, John 20
Pardue, R.M. 45
Parsons, Dr. Richard 60
Parsons, Margaret 148
Patriotic Fund 74, 90
Pearkes, George 116
Penhold Air Base 116, 118, 121, 123, 142, 150
Pentecostal Church of the Nazarene 61
Phenoix Lumber Company 105
Phillips, D.A. 124
Piper's Brickyard 44, 50, 52, 91
Piper, William 43
Playdon, Stan 125
Poole, Eric 110
Population 50, 59, 62, 102, 143, 147, 150, 153
Postill, William 49
Prehistory 7–8, 13–14
Presbyterian Church 47, 61
Presbyterian Missionary Society 37
Prohibition 70, 95–96
Provincial Training School 98, 103, 113, 141, 146, 149, 153
Public Works 52, 60, 64, 111, 140, 147
Purdy Opera House 50, 57

Queen Alexandra 53
Queen Elizabeth 113
Quota Club 111

Railroad Station 41, 58
Red Cross 81, 116, 118, 130
Red Deer Advocate (newspaper) 62, 65, 70, 73, 84, 87, 109, 128, 132, 150
Red Deer Aero Club 107
Red Deer Agricultural Society 44, 53, 83, 107
Red Deer Arena Company 99
Red Deer Athletic Association 139, 143
Red Deer Board of Trade 45, 47, 57, 60, 108, 130, 141
Red Deer Bottling 122
Red Deer Brick and Lumber Company 50
Red Deer Butter and Cheese Manufacturing Association 50
Red Deer Central Protestant School District No. 104 38
Red Deer Citizens Band 67, 70, 119
Red Deer Courthouse 51, 80, 103, *103*
Red Deer Creamery 46
Red Deer Crossing 26
Red Deer Echo (newspaper) 50
Red Deer Fair 44, 53, 60–61, 87–88, 105, 129, 130
Red Deer Fire Hall No. 1 53
Red Deer Full-Time Health Unit 105
Red Deer Golden Jubilee 154
Red Deer Golf Club 95
Red Deer Hockey Club 99
Red Deer Home Comforts Fund 124
Red Deer Horticultural Society 82
Red Deer Hospital 50–51, 60, 82, 93, *93*, 97, 138–139, 152, 153–154
Red Deer, incorporation 49, 62
Red Deer Junior College 151
Red Deer Ladies Hockey 53, 99
Red Deer Mill and Elevator Company 57
Red Deer Museum and Archives 96, *96*, 150, 153
Red Deer Mutual Telephone Company 111
Red Deer News (newspaper) 53, 67, 101–102
Red Deer Oil and Gas Company 64, 65
Red Deer, plan of (1890) 42
Red Deer, plan of (1947) 138
Red Deer Post Office 97, 141
Red Deer Public Library 68
Red Deer Rifle Association 44
Red Deer Salvage Committee 125
Red Deer School District (public) 45, 50, 55, 61, 100, 138, 144, 149
Red Deer School Division (county) 144, 149
Red Deer Separate School District 144
Red Deer, settlement 28–33, 41
Red Deer, streets 136–137
Red Deer Treasury Bills 75, 80, 82, 87, 91, 108, 110

Red Deer Women's Institute 81
Reinhart, Charles *125*
Reinholt Sandstone Quarry 47, *47*
Richards, Owen *125*
Richards, William 34
Riel, Louis 34
Riel Rebellion 34, 35–36, 155
Riverglen School 144, 149
Riverside Industrial Park 151
Roman Catholic Church 53, 55
Rosalind of Old Basing 60, *60*
Ross, Francis 69
Ross Street 86–87, *133, 134–135, 144*
Rotary Club 97, 99, 118
Rotary Picnic Park 29
Rotary Recreation Park 155
Royal Canadian Air Force 121
Royal Canadian Legion 122
Royal Canadian Mounted Police (RCMP) 107, 128, 150
Royal North West Mounted Police 83
Rundle, Robert Terrill 20

Sacred Heart Church 55, 101
Safeway 103
Salvation Army 81, 121
Saskatchewan Land and Homestead Company (SLHC) 28–29, 31, 33, 36, 44, 58, 62
Scott Fruit Company 98
Scott, Dennis *125*
Sharman, C.A. Julian 60
Shaw, F.D. 117
Smallpox epidemic 16, 22
Smethurst, Ken *125*
Smith, Charlie 26
Smith, George Wilbert 38, 92
Smith, Joseph 19
Smith, Zelma 96
Snider, W.N. 51
Social Credit Party 109–110, 112, 117, 129, 146
Soldiers Sanitorium 91, 98
Soldiers Settlement Board 91
Soldiers Wives Club 81
South Cottage School 61
South Hill School 144
South School 144
Speakman, Alfred 92, 117, 129
Sports and recreation 48, 53, 57, 80, 95, 98–99, 128–129, 130, 138–139, 141, 143–144
Square Garments Ltd. 60
St. Joseph's Convent 55, *56*, 61, 149
St. Laurent, Louis 144
St. Luke's Anglican Church 47, *47*
St. Mary's Aposotolic School 55, 90, 101
St. Mary's School (Montfort) 144
Stage coach service 30, 43
Stephenson, A.T. 57
Stephenson, Audrey 99

Stevenson–Hall Block 155
Stinson, Katherine *83*
Sutherland, Reverand Alexander 28

T. Eaton Company 101
Taylor, Ethel 148
The Castle (school) 55, *56*
The Crossing 26, *26*
The Old Crossing 43, 46, 108, 109, 113, 145
Thibeault, Father John Baptiste 20
Thompson, Babe 99
Thompson, David 16, 19, *19*
Thompson, Robert *152*
Town Council 49
Town Hall 53, 60
Treasury Branch 141
Trimble, A.H. 46
Twilight Lodge 146

United Dairies 122
United Farmers of Alberta 92, 109, 110
United Grain Growers Limited 88
Ure, David 130

V-E Day 132
V-J Day 132
Veterans Battalion 73
Veterans Day 87
Victorian Order of Nurses 51
Victory Fair 87
Victory Loan Campaigns 85, 122, 124, 126, 128
Vocational Training Centre 131–32
Voisin, Father Henri 53, 55
Vrooman, William A. 37, 38

W.E. Lord's 101
Waldbrooke, Maude 48, *48*
Waskasoo Park 60, 155
Welliver, R.B. 64
Wells, Ernie 99
Western General Electric Company 51, 57, 70, 71, 99
Western General Telephone Company 51, 76, 91
Whiskey trading 22
Wigwam Men's Club 80
Wilkins Hall 44
Wilkins Ranch 95
Windsor Hotel 74
Women's Christian Temperance Union (WCTU) 81
Women's suffrage 96
Wood, Kerry 110
Wood, Marjorie *110*
Woolsey, Thomas 20

Yakimchuck, Chuck *127*
Young Men's Christian Association (YMCA) 81, 121

The Colours of Red Deer

Canada Geese in flight

Aerial view of Red Deer, looking southwest

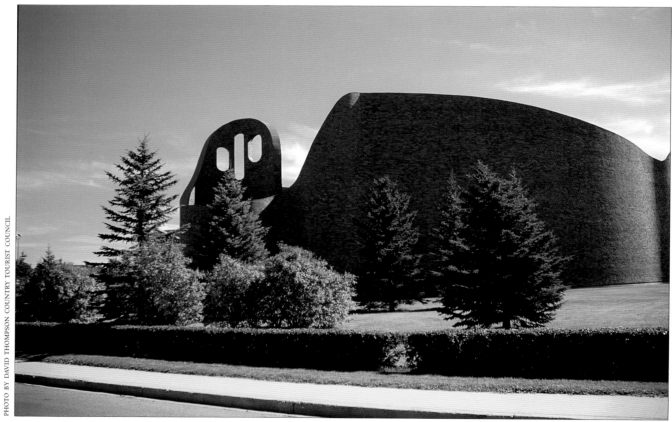

St. Mary's Church, designed by Douglas Cardinal

Fox family

Wildlife sightings are common in Red Deer's river valley

Autumn along Waskasoo Creek

Statue of Reverend Leonard Gaetz, Ross Street

Trees in winter

Making ice cream at Fort Normandeau

Woodpecker at feeder

The summertime beauty of City Hall Park

The Red Deer Royals entertain in Heritage Square

Red Deer and District Museum and Archives

Discovery Park at River Bend

Cronquist House, Beaver Ponds

The biking and walking trails in Waskasoo Park

Red Deer lies at the heart of a rich agricultural region

NOVA Chemicals Ltd. plant near Joffre